A COMMENTARY ON THE
Gospel
OF
Luke

Robert E. Obach
with
Albert Kirk

Paulist Press
New York/Mahwah

Nihil Obstat: Reverend John J. Jennings

Imprimatur: Most Rev. James H. Garland
             Auxiliary Bishop of the Archdiocese of Cincinnati

Date: November 16, 1985

The Nihil Obstat and Imprimatur are official declarations that a book or pamphlet is free of doctrinal or moral error. No implication is contained therein that those who have granted the Nihil Obstat and Imprimatur agree with the contents, opinions or statements expressed.

Scripture quotations in this book are from the *Good News Bible*, the Bible in Today's English Version. Copyright © American Bible Society 1966, 1971, 1976. Used by permission.

Library of Congress
Catalog Card Number: 85-62867

ISBN: 0-8091-2763-6

Published by Paulist Press
997 Macarthur Blvd.
Mahwah, New Jersey 07430

Printed and bound in the
United States of America

Contents

Preface

Luke tells the story of Jesus and his community in two parts: the Gospel and the Acts of the Apostles. These two books of the New Testament were intended to tell the story of Jesus' coming to his people and the story of the way his disciples brought his message to the world. Luke wrote for an audience that was primarily composed of Gentile Christians, our ancestors in the faith. It is likely that Luke's audience included Christians gathering in those churches that were related to the Church of Antioch, an early missionary center which sent out such missionaries as Barnabas and Paul (see Acts 13:1–3; 14:26–27).

Paul's perspective seems to have been one that saw as God's ultimate purpose the conversion of the Jews. In Paul's view, the entrance of the Gentiles into the believing community would make the Jewish people jealous and thereby lead them to accept Jesus as the Messiah (see Rom 11:13–15). Luke, however, goes beyond Paul's perspective. Luke realized that God's intention was to save the world through Jesus. Thus, in a very real sense, we can refer to Luke as the theologian of the one, holy, catholic and apostolic Church.

A Commentary on the Gospel of Luke is the last in the series of Paulist Press commentaries on the four accounts of the one Gospel of Jesus. The series had its beginnings in 1977 when Rev. Al Kirk and I were searching for a commentary on Matthew that would combine the insights from contemporary Scripture scholarship with a readable and popular style. We did not find such a commentary. Work-

1

ing with the experience of preparing more than four hundred persons to lead small groups desiring to study Matthew's account of the good news, we wrote *A Commentary on the Gospel of Matthew* for a diocesan-wide Lenten study in Memphis. Paulist Press subsequently published that work, followed by *A Commentary on the Gospel of John* (Kirk and Obach) and *A Commentary on the Gospel of Mark* (Terence J. Keegan, O.P.). *A Commentary on the Gospel of Luke* is based on the experience of preparing study leaders in both the diocese of Memphis and the archdiocese of Cincinnati.

This work on the Third Gospel is written in the hope of contributing to the building up of the body of Christ as we all continue the ministry of Jesus who proclaimed the kingdom of God in Galilee and Judea.

This commentary may be used in different ways. It may be a tool that helps the reader understand what Luke wanted to communicate. It may serve as an aid to prayer and meditation. It is hoped that this commentary on Luke's account will have its most positive effect when it is used as a tool for weekly, even daily study, accompanied by a periodic sharing of the meaning of the good news with others who are also seeking out the deepest meaning of the Third Gospel.

While Luke wrote to provide an "orderly account" (1:3), the Gospel is much more than an historical record; it is a living word. In the Gospel according to Luke, the Lord Jesus again speaks to his people. The words of the Gospel are addressed to each one of us insofar as we are all disciples of Jesus. In faith, we stand in continuity with those believing communities for whom the Third Gospel was first written.

Your goal, then, is a prayerful study of Luke's account of the good news of Jesus—"prayerful" because it is the

Holy Spirit who brings to life in each new generation the words of Jesus. Without the empowerment of the Spirit, we cannot hear the voice of the Lord speaking to us. It is a "prayerful study" because without intellectual effort the Gospel does not yield its rich abundance.

You are being asked to experience the Third Gospel, at first personally with the guidance of the Holy Spirit, and then, if possible, with others. Whether alone or with your study group, we suggest that you begin with a period of prayer. You may wish to make an act of faith that the Lord will speak to you, followed by a prayer invoking the inspiration of his Spirit.

During these eight weeks of study (or longer if desired) you may find it helpful to set aside a portion of each day to read, to reflect and to pray. Some may prefer several longer periods during the week in order to obtain a more comprehensive understanding of the material. Try to avoid a hasty reading of the Scripture passages and commentary just prior to the meeting of your study group. Spacing your reading of Scripture and commentary over a period of five days would allow a sixth day for reflecting on your week's readings and a seventh day for your group meeting.

None of us is able to open the Bible and understand its meaning as easily as one opens the newspaper and begins reading about what happened yesterday. Thus our first aim in writing this commentary is to provide you with a companion to the text of Luke's account of the Gospel. The English word "criticism" is derived from Greek terminology which refers to taking a deeper look into a literary work in order to appreciate the full meaning its author intended to communicate. So our study of Luke's version of the good news of Jesus will be enhanced by the tools of literary criticism that were first approved by Pope Pius XII (*Divino Afflante Spiritu*, 1943) and then by the bishops and Pope

Paul VI at the Second Vatican Council (*Dei Verbum*, 1964). Since the methods of literary criticism have been approved by our Church, we are pleased to be able to share the enriching insights of these tools of biblical scholarship with you in this commentary. We are convinced that they greatly contribute to our faith-filled hearing of the Gospel.

Our second goal in producing this commentary is to assist readers in applying the word of the Lord to the here and now of everyday living. Just as Luke took the traditions about Jesus and then explained their significance for his audience, so we, as individuals, or as believers in a study group, or as members of parish or diocese, have the opportunity to reflect on the words and deeds of Jesus and apply them to our own lives and to the building up of our parish or diocesan community.

These two goals might suggest a format for your study group meetings. The first portion of your meeting might deal with Luke's message in its original context. During this time the participants might concentrate on how Luke applied the teachings of Jesus to meet the needs of his own day. In the second portion, participants might strive to apply the Gospel to the situation in their own family, place of work, community and nation. Such a pattern respects the basic approach of God's revelation. Since God has chosen to speak to us through a human author, we must accurately understand what that author is saying so that we can effectively hear the word which God speaks to us today.

As I complete this work, I would like to express my gratitude to all those who have supported me in this endeavor. In particular I want to thank my friend, Rev. Al Kirk of the diocese of Memphis, for his editing and suggestions. A special word of thanks is given to Carroll T. Dozier, retired bishop of Memphis, who asked the people to reflect on the Third Gospel during the celebration of the tenth annniversary of the diocese in 1981. I am grateful to Sally Keyes and Carol Ann Cannon for critically reading portions of the manuscript, to Rev. Richard J. Cassidy of the archdiocese of Detroit for the insights offered through his book, *Jesus, Politics and Society*, to Rev. Ramond E. Brown, S.S., for his scholarly work contained in *The Birth of the Messiah*, and to Mrs. Mary Mahoney, who typed the edited manuscript. I want to acknowledge the encouragement given to me by my parents, George and Violet Obach, as I worked on portions of this book while enjoying their gracious hospitality. Finally, I thank my children, Noel Kevin, Jennifer Marie, Rebecca Ann and Sarah Elizabeth Carla, who receive a special mention here, for I carry a loving concern for them in all I do. Unless otherwise noted (NAB for New American Bible, JB for Jerusalem Bible), quotations from both the Hebrew and Christian Scriptures are taken from the fourth edition of *The Good News Bible*.

Week One

In this first week we will study the first two chapters of Luke's account of the Gospel. This material includes the evangelist's short preface, which explains his purpose for writing (1:1–4), and his understanding of the mission of Jesus, communicated to the reader through the traditions about the conceptions and births of John the Baptist and Jesus (1:5–2:42). The latter section is called the infancy narrative.

Contemporary biblical scholarship points out that the infancy narrative was developed after the traditions regarding ministry, passion and resurrection were firmly in place. Thus the material in Luke 1:5–2:52 provides us with a miniature portrait of the entire Gospel. The finding of Jesus in the temple (2:41–52) clearly illustrates the way in which an incident contained in the infancy narrative summarizes the public life of Jesus.

The Holy Spirit's activity is central to the story contained in chapters 1 and 2. The power of the Spirit fills and inspires all those who, directly or indirectly, encounter the child described as Savior, Christ and Lord (2:11). Mary, the one upon whom the Spirit comes to rest, has a fundamental role in the events surrounding Jesus' conception and birth. Luke portrays her as the model disciple, for she is the one who will trust in God's saving power from the moment of the annuniciation of Jesus' conception to the time when the Spirit comes to the community of disciples on Pentecost (see 1:38; Acts 1:14 and 2:4).

7

DAILY STUDY ASSIGNMENTS: WEEK ONE

Day	Luke	Commentary
1	1:1–4	pp. 10–12
2	1:5–38	pp. 14–21
3	1:39–80	pp. 21–25
4	2:1–21	pp. 25–31
5	2:22–52	pp. 31–36

6 Review Luke 1:1–2:52 in light of the reflection questions that follow.

7 Group meets for study and sharing.

1. Share with the members of your group the expectations you have as you undertake this study of the Third Gospel.

2. What does Luke's preface (1:1–4) tell us about his reasons for writing his account of the Gospel?

3. What kind of process did Luke probably use to write his "orderly account"?

4. In terms of the themes that Luke wanted to stress, what is the significance of Mary's canticle (1:46–55)? What is the significance of the announcement of Jesus' birth being made to shepherds?

5. Share with one another how the canticles, the events reported and the persons involved in the infancy narrative help to point out that Jesus is the fulfillment of the hopes of the Jewish people.

6. What are some of the ways in which the infancy narrative is better understood when it is seen in connection with the rest of Luke's account of the Gospel?

7. How can the finding of Jesus in the temple (2:41–52) be seen as a miniature portrait of the Gospel as a whole?

Luke's Preface, 1:1–4

In one long, carefully constructed sentence Luke explains the purpose of his work to Theophilus (1:1–4). Because "Theophilus" literally means "lover of God," some commentators understand Theophilus as the symbolic name for the Christian believer about to read Luke's account of the good news. Other commentators are of the opinion that Theophilus was a particular person, most likely Luke's patron, a person who had the means to see that this literary work was copied and distributed to others.

Luke begins with the acknowledgement that other persons have already written accounts of things Jesus had done (1:1–2). Among the accounts that Luke referred to is the Gospel according to Mark, the first writer to combine both the words and the deeds of Jesus into a narrative format. Prior to Mark's effort there were various "oral traditions" which related some of the words and deeds of Jesus, and there were also some written collections of the sayings of Jesus. Luke himself will use all these—the oral traditions, a written collection of Jesus' sayings and the Gospel account written by Mark. Those who wrote and those who passed on the traditions had received their information from witnesses "who saw these things from the beginning and who proclaimed the message" (1:2).

In his account Luke will introduce the men and women who are the eye-witnesses of the events in Jesus' life, death, resurrection and ascension. Luke's explicit purpose is to write an "orderly account" for Theophilus in order that he might have "the full truth about everything" he has been taught (1:3–4). It is likely that Theophilus had been instructed in the Christian faith. Perhaps Luke wanted to present to both Theophilus and other newly instructed or insufficiently instructed Christians a view of Jesus so that they could come to a deeper faith in him as Savior, Messiah and Lord (see 2:11). Luke's purpose is clearly evangelical; he writes so that others will come to a wholehearted belief in Jesus.

To achieve his evangelical purpose Luke has "carefully studied all these matters from their beginning" in order to write a fully researched account of the origins of the believing community's faith in Jesus (1:3). One of Luke's basic sources is the Gospel account of Mark. Written some twenty years earlier, Mark's version is stark and abrupt. With a keen awareness of the persecution of Roman Christians by the Emperor Nero in the 60s, Mark stressed the passion of Jesus, the centrality of the cross, and the nearness of the final coming of Jesus. It is possible that Mark was aware of the impending destruction of Jerusalem which he viewed as a sign of the end of the world. The reader of Mark's account was left with the impression that the world would soon perish. Mark had left little room for history, little space for the development of the Church in this world. It seems that Luke wanted to relate the good news of Jesus in such a way that it would help believers to live the kind of life in which faith is integrated with daily existence. Realizing that there would probably be a long period between Jesus' ascension and his return in glory at the end of time, Luke wrote his two-part work, the Gospel and the Acts of the Apostles. In these two volumes Luke told his audience about Jesus and about the new period that had begun in world history—the era of the Church.

Besides Mark, Luke incorporated other sources into his account. One such source was a written collection of the sayings of Jesus known by biblical scholars as the Q document. This collection of sayings had been in circulation for some time, for we know that Matthew also used the Q document as one of the sources for his account of the good news. Another source is Luke's own special tradition, a source of information not available to Mark or Matthew. In the infancy narrative the account of the birth of John the Baptist, the picture of Jesus being born in a stable and being visited by shepherds, the story of the presentation of Jesus in the temple and the narration of the finding of Jesus in the temple are all derived from Luke's unique source(s).

It was Luke's major task to select information from his sources and work out one orderly and contemporary account of the Gospel. We can imagine Luke seated at a table, with the Gospel of Mark at his right, the scroll with the sayings of Jesus on his left, and Luke's notes from his special sources in still another place. Luke then goes about the work of joining these various incidents and sources and making of them an harmonious whole. When he is finished, Theophilus and the other believers will have an account of the good news of Jesus that affirms "everything which you have been taught" (1:4).

The Infancy Narrative, 1:5–2:52

OVERVIEW. Until the 1960s most Catholics regarded the material found in the first two chapters of Luke's Gospel (called the infancy narrative by biblical scholars) as if it were the same kind of writing as the account of the ministry, death and resurrection of Jesus found in the rest of the Gospel. Biblical scholars, however, had already begun to see that the account of the birth of Jesus and of the events leading up to it had an origin quite different from the narrative about his ministry.

Thus, a second phase in the understanding of the infancy narrative developed. The account of the origin and birth of Jesus was studied as an independent unit that could be detached from the rest of the Gospel, because it was recognized that the infancy narrative was written in a special literary form. Special attention was paid to determine the historical accuracy of the infancy narrative. Scholars searched for historical evidence of a census in King Herod's domain or the appearance of a star at the time of Jesus' birth, but they could not find proof for these events.

In recent years we have moved into a third phase in the approach of scholarship to the infancy narrative, an approach that greatly aids our understanding of the significance of these chapters. The key question to be asked is this: What was Luke's purpose in placing the infancy narrative in his Gospel account? As we shall see, the answer is that the events surrounding Jesus' conception and birth form a miniature account of the good news which is proclaimed in the main portion of the Gospel. Thus, the significance of the infancy narrative can be appreciated most fully when it is seen bathed in the light of the whole ministry of Jesus, beginning with the preaching of John the Baptist (3:2) and concluding with Jesus' ascension (24:51).

The infancy narrative functions like the overture of a Broadway musical. The overture may be the first music that the audience hears, but in fact it contains only brief themes that are taken from the music that will be played during the total production. So it is with the Lucan presentation of Jesus' origins. The narrative of Jesus' conception and birth is actually based on his ministry, passion and resurrection-ascension.

Furthermore, because Luke is writing for an audience that is primarily Gentile, he tries to provide these new believers with the background that formed the Jewish environment of Jesus. Thus, the infancy narrative functions as a dramatic bridge linking the Hebrew Scriptures with God's new deed—the event of Jesus. The infancy narrative both presupposes and incorporates the experience of the Hebrew people from the call of Abram (Gen 12:1) to the appearance of John the Baptist in the wilderness (3:2). Note as you study this section how Luke quietly integrates into his prologue events which remind us of the great heroes and heroines of the Jewish faith. Thus alerted, we can glimpse the towering figures of Abraham and his childless wife Sarah behind Luke's account of Zechariah and Elizabeth (1:5–25). Throughout the infancy narrative Luke brings out the continuity that exists between the story of Israel and the story of Jesus.

The Annunciation of the Birth of John the Baptist, 1:5–25

COMMENTARY. Luke begins his story in God's special city of Jerusalem. At the evening hour of sacrifice, Zechariah enters the temple, the central focus of the religious life of the Jewish people. Because there were thousands of priests, most of whom earned their living as tradesmen and farmers in the city and countryside around Jerusalem, Zechariah would have had very few opportunities to enter the innermost place of the temple, the place where the altar of sacrifice stood. Luke notes that both he and his wife Elizabeth are from priestly families and that both are devout in their faith, observers of the whole law (1:6). They are also childless and, because of their advanced years, without hope of conceiving. In view of Luke's stress on the theme of prophecy fulfilled, both have significant names. In Hebrew Zechariah means "Yahweh remembers" and Elizabeth means "God has sworn."

It is important to realize that Luke is not a reporter writing an article for *Time* magazine. He wants his readers to remember the broader context of Israel's history. The deeper significance of Zechariah and Elizabeth is to be found in the way their story summarizes the story of Israel. We can take the meaning of their names and ask: What is it that God has sworn and remembered?

The first person to whom God spoke regarding a covenant was Abraham (see Gen 15 and 17). Abraham and Sarah were both childless and very old (Gen 18:11–12). Yet with God's intervention Sarah conceived and gave birth to Isaac, the child in whom the nation of Israel had its beginnings. The point is that God blessed Abraham and Sarah with a child at precisely that time when there was no longer any natural expectation. Therefore, when Luke begins his Gospel account with an elderly and childless couple, we find an underlying statement about God's giving new beginnings through a couple who no longer have any common-sense expectation of conceiving a child. At this very moment God sends his messenger Gabriel to announce to Zechariah that his wife will conceive a child who shall herald the beginnings of a new Israel (1:15–17). Gabriel's announcement about John underscores the joy not only of his parents but also of the whole covenant people. John is linked with the great leaders of Israel. For example, the abstention from wine and strong drink connects John with Sampson, the charismatic leader raised up by God to lead his people out of oppression (Jgs 13:2–7). As all of those whom God has used to restore his people, John will be filled with the Holy Spirit. The reference to Elijah (1:17) links John with Malachi, the last of Israel's prophets. The final sentence at the end of the scroll of the prophetic writings speaks of God's promise to send again his prophet Elijah in order to reconcile the children of Israel with their fathers (Mal 3:24).

Verses 18–20 are variously interpreted. On the one hand, the text indicates that Zechariah is at fault because he asks for a sign instead of accepting Gabriel's message. His request for an additional sign is granted, but not in the way he expected. Zechariah is struck dumb, rendered incapable of speaking about God's gracious acts until the day on which his son is named with the name given by God (see 1:63–64).

On the other hand, some scholars point out that Luke is structuring this account along the lines of the literary pattern found in the story of Daniel. Perhaps the speechlessness of Daniel (Dan 10:15) is the model Luke follows in presenting this episode involving Zechariah. We twentieth century readers need to be reminded that the ancient ways of writing differ considerably from those of our own day. We tend to ask the question, "Did it happen like this or not?" But the people who wrote in biblical times did not write to answer such a one-dimensional question. The ancients wanted to explore the relationships between past, present and future. So their writings answer multi-dimensional questions. They were more concerned with questions like "Does it continue to happen?" and "Will it happen in the future?" than they were with the question "Did it happen?" Luke's purpose is to show that God's way of revealing his loving care is recognizable because it happens over and over again. If God acted in such a way in the past, he will do so again in the future.

The Annunciation of the Birth of Jesus, 1:26–38

OVERVIEW. There are only two accounts of the circumstances surrounding Jesus' conception and birth, Matthew's and Luke's. While these accounts differ in many details, there seems to be a common tradition on which both were based: an angelic announcement that Jesus would be the Messiah of David's family and that Jesus was conceived by Mary who was a virgin. Matthew takes this tradition and fashions it in such a way as to meet the needs of his persecuted community. Luke begins with the same tradition and fashions it into a narrative which can proclaim the good news to a Gentile audience.

Matthew begins his infancy narrative with the genealogy of Jesus, then explains "how the birth of Jesus Christ took place" (Mt 1:18). When Luke tells the story, he seeks to clarify the relationship between Jesus and John the Baptist. (John's disciples are still proclaiming that their martyred leader was the Messiah. Luke wants to acknowledge the greatness of John and the validity of his prophetic ministry. At the same time he wants to demonstrate clearly that John is subordinate to Jesus.) Luke accomplishes this clarification by the structure of these two chapters. He begins with the two announcements of the birth of John and Jesus, which he follows with the accounts of the two holy births.

As you study the two annunciations, you will note many similarities. In both accounts Gabriel appears with a message from God which troubles the recipient. The angel carefully explains the importance of both John and Jesus in God's saving plan, which evokes a question from both Zechariah and Mary. After Gabriel's response, both receive a sign that the message indeed comes from God. By reading Genesis 17:1–19 you can see how Luke has designed his two birth announcements along the lines of the revelation to Abraham of Isaac's birth.

While the details in these parallel accounts are significant, the differences are even more significant. Zechariah and Elizabeth were from priestly families (1:5), but Joseph belongs to the royal family of David (1:27). From David's line would come the Messiah who would bring peace and justice to God's people (see Is 9:5–7, 11:1–9). Zechariah and Elizabeth conceived a child in the ordinary way, even though their advanced age made the birth remarkable. Mary is a young woman, a virgin betrothed to Joseph. Her conceiving is totally unique. It is unprecedented and unparalleled in Israel's history. Jesus is conceived without an earthly father, an event that had never been a part of Israel's expectations or experience. One last difference: in the splendid temple in Jerusalem the priest Zechariah doubts the message of God's angel, while in the obscure town of Nazareth a young woman declares her trustful willingness to be the humble servant of God.

The Good News Bible chooses to translate the angel's greeting to Mary in everyday language: "Peace be with you!" This wording follows the traditional Latin text, "Ave Maria," from which we take the wording of the familiar prayer, "Hail Mary." The Greek text can also be translated in more formal language, as does *The New American Bible:* "Rejoice, O highly favored daughter!" This wording enables us to hear the words of the prophet Zephaniah, which must have resounded in Luke's mind and heart as he wrote:

> *Rejoice, O highly favored daughter! The Lord is with you.*
> *Blessed are you among women (1:28, NAB).*

The presence of the Lord with his people and his victory, foretold by Zephaniah, will now be fulfilled in the birth of Jesus!

Mary does not understand the scope of the angel's message (1:29) and so the good news is clarified. Once again God will take the initiative and graciously enter the lives of his covenant people to deliver them. (Note that Jesus in Hebrew means "Yahweh saves.") Mary's son will be "the Son of the Most High God" (1:32).

As we read that Jesus will also be a king, we remember the promise God made to David through the prophet Nathan. That promise was linked with David's desire to build God a house, that is, a temple. This temple would replace the tent of the Lord's presence in which the ark of the covenant rested (Ex 40:1ff). Nathan declared to David that God had different plans. Instead of David building a house for the Lord, God would build David a house, that is, a dynasty, a family from which would come an everlasting ruler of the people (2 Sam 7:11–16). Because Mary is about to conceive the Son of the Most High by the power of the Holy Spirit of God, the text suggests that she is about to become God's new temple, the tent of the Lord's presence, the very dwelling place of God. Puzzled, Mary refers to her maidenhood and asks, " 'How, then, can this be?' " In Gabriel's answer we discover another aspect of the biblical theme regarding God's dwelling place. The angel's declaration that God's power would rest upon (overshadow) Mary reminds us of the conclusion of the Book of Exodus:

Then the cloud covered the Tent and the dazzling light of the Lord's presence filled it (Ex 40:34).

The child Mary was about to conceive would be called "the Son of God" (1:35). As a sign of the truth of his words, Gabriel declares that the barren Elizabeth is now in the sixth month of her pregnancy. That is the tangible proof that God can do all things, including the bestowal of motherhood upon a young virgin named Mary (1:37).

Mary consents: "May it happen to me as you have said" (1:38). Her "let-it-be," her *fiat*, changes human history.

There is a deep Christological statement being made in this story of the annunciation: there never was a single instant of Jesus' life in which he was not intimately related to God. From the time of his conception Jesus could be called "the Son of the Most High God" (1:32, 35). Unlike the conceptions of Isaac, Sampson and John the Baptist, all of whom were conceived naturally in spite of the great age of their parents, Jesus had no earthly father. Jesus was conceived by the power of God alone. There are no parallels in salvation history, no Jewish expectations of a Messiah who would be conceived without the seed of a man. Jesus is the free and total gift of God. He is pure gift—no strings attached.

REFLECTION. It is to Mary's everlasting honor that she gave her consent to be the mother of the one who was sent by God. But remember that these incidents found in the infancy narrative presuppose that the whole life of Jesus had been lived, proclaimed and written about before Luke wrote this prologue. We do not know how Mary understood her assent. It is likely that she had only a vague perception of the future. Perhaps that is why Luke pictures her as one who pondered over the events of Jesus' childhood (2:19, 51). The Gospel text clearly tells us that Mary and Joseph "did not understand" what Jesus meant when he spoke with them at the age of twelve (2:50).

If Mary did not know the details of the future, and yet Mary nevertheless said "yes" to God, then Mary is one of us. We are called to make a commitment to God without knowing the future. Thus Mary becomes a model of the authentic disciple. Moreover, if the criterion for discipleship is doing the will of God (see 8:21), then Mary becomes the first disciple of Jesus (1:38).

Yes, Mary is unique in that she fashioned the flesh of Jesus in her womb. But Mary also represents all future disciples of Jesus, for they are called to manifest Jesus in the flesh of their own lives. The way Mary freely responded so long ago becomes the model for all of us who are addressed as disciples of Jesus.

Mary Visits Elizabeth, 1:39–56

As we are coming to expect, Luke's account of Mary's journey to Judea is told on two levels of meaning. On the obvious level we hear of a simple act of kindness, as Mary hurries off to assist her elderly cousin and share the joy of their miraculous conceptions. On another level of meaning, we discover again the ways in which these events introduce a new age for God's people. Prior to the public appearance of John there was in Israel a tradition that there had been a drought of God's Spirit. For hundreds of years there had been no acknowledged prophet, and many believed that God had withheld his Spirit because of the hard-heartedness of his people. Looking back from his perspective in the 80s, Luke sees the Spirit being poured out on everyone associated with Jesus. Thus, when Mary, having conceived Jesus through the power of the Spirit, approaches her kinswoman, Elizabeth is also filled with the Holy Spirit. Once again inspired prophecy pours forth. Elizabeth joyfully proclaims that both Mary and the child she bears are deeply blessed (2:42).

Mary responds with her canticle of the reign of God, known to us as the *Magnificat*. This inspired prayer is an important part of Luke's "overture" in which he gives his readers a preview of the main themes of the Gospel. Thus, Mary's prayer speaks of the great reversals that happen because of God's concern for the poor and lowly. These themes are at the core of Jesus' message. He will bring the good news to the poor; he will set free the oppressed (4:18–21). What is happening in Mary's life as she carries Jesus in her womb is foreshadowing what her son will do during his future ministry.

Mary's beautiful canticle summarizes the Hebrew Scriptures in a wonderful way. Note how it gathers together the great themes of Israel's history—joy in God's powerful deeds on behalf of his people; the holiness of the One who is at the same time most merciful; the special compassion of God for the poor and lowly; his fidelity to the chosen people. As Luke unfolds his Gospel, it becomes clear to those who trust, as did Mary (1:45), in God's faithfulness.

REFLECTION. Luke's account of Mary's prayer of praise (1:46–55) manifests one of his special themes—God's loving concern for the poor and powerless. Living in our American culture, with its emphasis on owning things and getting ahead, it is difficult for us to appreciate what Luke is trying to communicate here. Perhaps it is helpful to search out both what Luke is and is not saying. He is not advocating the indigence of poverty as the Christian ideal. He is not stating that material possessions are evil. Luke is well aware of the fact that the believing community must live in history; he does not think that the end of the world is swiftly approaching (as Mark seems to assume). Luke knows that the disciple of Jesus is called to live in this world and all that such living implies—earning a living, buying and selling, providing for family and extended family. But Luke also knows that God cares for all people, particularly the poor and the oppressed. In the beginning of the Gospel, in Mary's prayer of praise, Luke is stating what Jesus lived and taught.

Luke seems to have been aware that many of his readers had better than average incomes. In the Third Gospel we find much advice for those in positions of leadership. It may have been the case that many Christians became leaders because they owned homes large enough to accommodate the Christian community when its members gathered to celebrate the Eucharist. In those days, a town or section of a city might have a "local church" of about fifty or sixty adults. There were few large public buildings for the worshiping community until the fourth century, the time when the Roman state first recognized Christianity as a religion. Reading between the lines, we sense that those Christians who were economically better off were biased against those who were poor. Mary's prayer of praise indicates that God gives salvation to all, especially to the nobodies of society. Thus Mary's song overturns the values of the world. She expresses her praise of the God who topples the mighty of this world and who lifts the poor and oppressed to high places.

The Birth of John the Baptist, 1:57–80

Luke describes the birth of John and the events surrounding it in such a way as to emphasize God's fidelity to his people. The scene is alive with one of his favorite themes: joy in God's goodness and mercy. Thus, when Zechariah asserts that the name of the child is John (God is gracious), he recovers his ability to speak and begins to praise God (1:64). The question asked by the people— "What is this child going to be?"—prepares us for Zechariah's canticle. Filled with the Holy Spirit, Zechariah prophetically announces what God has done (1:69–75) and then foretells what God will do in the future (1:76–79).

It is helpful in studying Zechariah's canticle to recognize what can be called "the prophetic technique." The prophetic speaker frequently projects himself into the future. From that perspective the prophet proclaims the future acts of God as if they had already taken place. For example, even though Jesus has not yet been born, Zechariah speaks of God as having already provided a mighty Savior who is a descendant of David (1:69).

Like Mary's prayer of praise, Zechariah's canticle gathers together the key themes found in the Hebrew Scriptures. The second movement of the canticle (1:76–79) answers the question raised by the people about the kind of child John will be (1:66). He is to be the herald of the Most High God. Verse 76 is based on the text of Isaiah 40:3, the announcement that God's angels would prepare a road through the desert from Babylon to Israel. On this road God's chosen people traveled from their Babylonian captivity (587–539 B.C.) to their homeland. Many centuries later, Zechariah foresees that his son John will serve in a similar way. As God's herald, John prepares for the new saving deed that will take place in Jesus.

This salvation will occur through the Lord's forgiving the sins of his people (1:77). In this way another keynote of Jesus' ministry, the forgiveness of sins, is sounded. As Luke will point out, Jesus travels from north to south preaching the forgiveness of sins. Jesus goes to his death uttering his dying prayer, "Forgive them, Father! They do not know what they are doing" (23:34).

Luke concludes this scene by referring to John's full development as a person: "The child grew . . . in body and spirit" (1:80). The reference to his living in the desert until the time of his public appearance may indicate that his parents entrusted him to the Essene community at Qumran, located in the desert region west of the Dead Sea.

The Birth and Circumcision of Jesus, 2:1–21

OVERVIEW. Just as Luke composed parallel accounts of the annunciations of John and Jesus, he did the same with the birth stories. Placed side by side, the key elements of Luke's parallel stories are as follows:

The birth of John	1:57	The birth of Jesus	2:6–7
Joy at John's birth	1:58	Joy at Jesus' birth	2:10
Circumcision and proclamation of John's purpose	1:59–80	Circumcision and proclamation of Jesus' purpose	2:11, 21–38
Canticle	1:68–79	Canticle	2:29–32
Conclusion: growth of John to manhood	1:80	Conclusion: growth of Jesus into manhood	2:40

It is possible that the material found in chapter 1 was originally a tradition that was unconnected with the material found in what we call chapter 2. The story of Jesus' birth and presentation in the temple does not build on the subject matter of the first chapter. Thus we have a new introduction that begins with a census called by the emperor; there is no mention of John the Baptist; Mary and Joseph are introduced as if nothing had been mentioned of them prior to their appearance in Bethlehem (2:4–6). Rather than being aware of the nature and mission of her child, Mary is depicted as one trying to discern the meaning of the events regarding the circumstances of Jesus birth (2:19, 51). Some scholars surmise that Luke had access to two different traditions which he subsequently spliced together as he wrote his "orderly account" for Theophilus (1:3).

The material in chapter 2 has three distinguishable units: the birth of Jesus (2:1–21), the presentation of Jesus in the temple (2:22–39), and the "finding" of Jesus in the temple at the age of twelve (2:41–51). The third unit appears to be yet another tradition which was incorporated into the infancy narrative after it had been completed.

COMMENTARY. While John the Baptist had been linked with Herod, the secular ruler of Judea (1:5), Jesus has a far more solemn introduction into human history. He is born in the reign of Caesar Augustus, Roman emperor from 30 B.C. to 14 A.D. Because he had brought peace to an empire ravaged by civil war, Augustus had been acknowledged as "the savior of the world." Luke, both by associating Jesus' birth with the Roman ruler and by the angels' message (2:11–14), asserts that Jesus is the authentic Savior of the world, for it is he who brings true peace to humankind.

The mention of the census has a double function. First, it indicates that the parents of Jesus are obedient citizens of the empire, an important assertion at a time when the followers of Jesus were suspect in virtue of their beliefs and non-participation in Roman religious practices. Second, the census explains why Jesus was born in Bethlehem when Nazareth was known to be his home. Mary and Joseph came to Bethlehem because the census required people to register in the city of their origin. Joseph, a descendant of David, is linked with "the birthplace of King David" (2:4).

To appreciate the significance of the birth of Jesus—the Christmas story—it is more important to consider the evangelist's message than to gather statistics or "facts." The reason this is so is that we do not have the facts; we only have the message. For example, a brief comparison of the birth accounts according to Matthew and according to Luke will show that Matthew thought of Mary and Joseph as living in a house in Bethlehem (Mt 2:11) while Luke writes of Jesus being born in a stable and returning home to Nazareth after forty days (Lk 2:7, 39). Matthew depicts the parents of Jesus traveling to Egypt and then settling in Nazareth to avoid endangerment from Herod's son (Mt 2:16–23).

While the details differ, there are important structural parallels in both infancy narratives. Both accounts speak of an angelic annunciation made to one of Jesus' parents. Both speak of a divine manifestation of the birth of Jesus to a special audience. While Matthew tells of a star leading Gentile astrologers to Jesus (Mt 2:1–11), Luke relates that an angel proclaimed the birth of the Messiah to shepherds (2:8–11). In each case the announcement to the special audience tells us something that manifests the mission of Jesus. In Matthew the pagan astrologers symbolize that the Gentiles are included in the salvation Jesus brings to the world. In Luke we are told that Jesus comes to grace the lives of the poor and powerless, aptly represented by the shepherds. They are the ones to first hear that Jesus is "Christ the Lord" (2:11).

When the time came for Mary to deliver her child, she "gave birth to her first son" (2:7). By asserting that Jesus is Mary's "first son," Luke is not enunciating the Roman Catholic belief in Mary's perpetual virginity, nor is he denying this belief (as some Protestant Christians claim). Rather, Luke wants to assert that in the Jewish understanding of inheritance, Jesus is the heir to David's throne (see 1 Sam 7:16).

The description of the newborn child being laid in a manger because "there was no room for them to stay in the inn" (2:7) has nothing to do with an alleged hard-hearted innkeeper. Luke wants to emphasize that Jesus is placed in a manger, a detail mentioned three times in this episode (2:7, 12, 16). The reference to the manger probably refers to Isaiah's prophetic indictment of Israel:

> *Hear, O heavens, and listen, O earth,*
> *for the Lord speaks:*
> *Sons have I raised and reared,*
> *but they have disowned me!*
> *An ox knows its owner,*
> *and an ass, its master's manger;*
> *But Israel does not know,*
> *my people has not understood (Is 1:2–3, NAB).*

The shepherds, representing the humblest of Israel, recognize the manger of their Lord (2:12, 15). That is the point. The announcement to the shepherds anticipates an important theme of Jesus' ministry and message. The manger symbolizes acceptance by a few and rejection by many of God's chosen people. Those who do accept Jesus, the ones who do hear his message, are the outcasts of society, the poor, the oppressed, the despised, and the sinners. We often miss the depth of power in Luke's narration because we have an overly sentimental or romanticized view of shepherds. We need to realize that in the time of Jesus shepherds had no social or religious status. They were often associated with thieves, were poor as dirt and unwashed as well. From the religious perspective they were regarded as incapable of keeping the law, habitually breaking the sabbath as they cared for their flocks seven days a week. For these reasons it is a most unexpected and amazing event that shepherds are the first to hear the "good news" that brings "great joy to all the people" (2:10). The shepherds—the poor, despised nobodies—are told that *their Savior* has come:

> *This very day in David's town your Savior was born—Christ the Lord (2:11).*

As the shepherds tell their story to the parents of the child found in the manger, Mary has two responses. She, like Joseph, is amazed (2:16–18); she also began to think deeply about "these things" (2:19). The term "these things" is Luke's shorthand way of referring to all the events of Jesus' life. Luke began his Gospel by referring to those "who saw these things from the beginning" (1:2), and then, in one of the final scenes of the Gospel, he will depict the two disciples walking to Emmaus while talking about "all the things that had happened" (24:14). With the inspiration of the Spirit and with all his skill as an author, Luke continues to portray Mary as the model for all disciples of Jesus. She, we must remember, is the one person who is present both at the birth of Jesus and at Pentecost (Acts 1:14). Mary, the disciple, is completely open to the presence of God in her life, expecting God to be at work within her. She does not always immediately understand the ways of God but treasures the events which surround the birth and ministry of her son and ponders continually their meaning.

With the departure of the shepherds, this scene concludes (2:20). Like every Israelite male, Jesus is circumcised on the eighth day. On his body he bears the sign of belonging to the covenanted people:

Your name will no longer be Abram, but Abraham. . . . Each
one must be circumcised, and this will be a physical sign to
show that my covenant with you is everlasting (Gen 17:5,
13).

REFLECTION. In Luke's second volume, the Acts of the
Apostles, we read of Peter's declaration on Pentecost that
God had raised Jesus and had made him "Lord and Messiah" (Acts 2:36). This declaration can serve as an example
of how the Church's understanding of Jesus developed
through the decades of the first century. What were, at one
time, titles for the risen Jesus, as seen in Peter's declaration, were later applied to earlier portions of Jesus' life. In
Luke 2:11 the Church's understanding of Jesus is projected
back to Jesus as an infant. In this one verse Luke uses three
of the most significant Christological titles: Savior, Christ
and Lord. "Savior" is a title that speaks of what he does for
each of us. "Christ" sums up the Jewish hope for God's
Messiah. "Lord" signifies that Jesus is of God, that Jesus is
divine. But it is "Savior" that is for Luke the most significant title for Jesus. Salvation is one of the core themes of
Luke's account, and he uses the verb form of "to save"
thirty times in his two volume work, the Gospel and Acts.
    There is nothing that needs to be shocking about the
movement that takes the titles for the risen Jesus to the giving of these titles to the infant Jesus. The development in
the Church's understanding of Jesus seems to take place in
our own individual relationship with him. Our relationship with him is dynamic and must grow and deepen as
we change and mature. Our friendship and commitment
to him grows as we perceive more clearly who Jesus is.
What we understood as a seven year old first communicant
changed by the time we became teenagers, and continued
to change through our thirties, fifties, and seventies. This

is as it should be, for no relationship can remain the same. Each relationship, each friendship, each marriage is between two persons who freely choose to sustain their mutual involvement as they go through the numerous transitions of human living. The same can be said of our relationship with Jesus. It grows, declines, revives, endures, distances, dies and rises.

The Presentation of Jesus in the Temple, 2:22–40

COMMENTARY. Although Christian tradition has tended to overlook its importance, Luke may have intended the presentation of Jesus in the temple to be the climax of his infancy narrative. The birth, circumcision and presentation are closely related, and the third aspect is crucial, for it takes place in Jerusalem, the city of salvation. Mary and Joseph bring Jesus to the temple, the place where God's special presence dwells. The Hebrew Scriptures speak of Israel's longing for God to come to his people. When Simeon sees the son of Mary, he speaks of Jesus as "the glory of your people Israel" (2:32, JB). Luke follows this by including the Gentiles with the Jewish people: Jesus is a light who will reveal God's will to the Gentiles (2:32). In Luke's wording we hear an echo of the second of Isaiah's four "suffering servant" poems:

> The Lord said to me, "I have a greater task for you, my servant. Not only will you restore to greatness the people of Israel . . . but I will also make you a light to the nations" (Is 49:6).

As Luke continues the Gospel the importance of Jesus' fulfillment of the suffering servant poems will become clear.

Here Luke points that Jesus comes to bring into existence a new messianic people constituted of both Jews and Gentiles.

The words of the prophet Malachi also form the background for the presentation of Jesus. Clearly Luke wants his readers to understand that Jesus fulfills the prophecy of Malachi:

> I will send my messenger to prepare the way for me. Then the Lord you are looking for will suddenly come to his Temple" (Mal 3:1).

By his arrival in the temple Jesus begins the long awaited messianic era. In 2:22–24 Luke refers to two different observances of the law: the purification ritual for a mother (22:22a and 2:24) and the dedication of the first-born to the Lord (2:22b and 2:23). The Mosaic legislation in Leviticus 12:3–8 requires that the mother be made "ritually clean from her loss of blood" (Lv 12:5). Menstruation or childbirth was thought of as a loss of vitality, for the Jews thought of life as contained in the blood. Such a loss was restored by ritual prayers or offerings. Mary's purification expresses her willing obedience to the Mosaic law. In verses 22, 23 and 27 Luke indicates that Mary and Joseph were faithful and observant Jews. The offering of the two doves (2:24) was the gift of those who were too poor to afford the sacrifice of a lamb (Lv 12:8).

The presenting of the first-born son and his redemption (buying back) were also required by the Mosaic law (Ex 13:2–16; Num 18:15ff). While Mary and Joseph "present" or "dedicate" Jesus to God, note that they do not "redeem," that is, symbolically buy back Jesus (2:23). This is another way of stating that Jesus always belonged to his heavenly Father. The same theme will soon be found on the lips of the twelve year old Jesus: "Didn't you know that I had to be in my Father's house?" (2:49). Simeon's canticle is the fourth song of praise found in the infancy narrative. At the end of his long life Simeon declares, "Now, Lord . . . you may let your servant go in peace" (2:29). Simeon appears here as a representative of Israel's yearning for the arrival of the Messiah. Led by the Spirit, Simeon recognizes that Jesus comes to save both Jew and Gentile. The salvation of the world rests in the infant he holds in his arms.

Simeon blesses the amazed parents, then addresses Mary alone, telling her of the mission of Jesus and the sword of sorrow that will break her heart (2:34–35). The prophecy foreshadows the opposition that Jesus will face during his public ministry. Since Mary will live to see her son rejected and crucified, deep grief will be hers. For Mary, the model disciple, as for all those associated closely with Jesus, discipleship is costly.

There is one more witness, Anna, a prophetess whose deep commitment to God is manifested in her worship, fasting and prayer. Like Sarah, Miriam, Deborah, Hannah, and the other Jewish women who lived with deep faith, Anna recognizes God's intervention in history. Thus she thanks God and speaks to those who were waiting for God to set Jerusalem free (2:38). Jerusalem represents Israel and "waiting" is the posture of those receiving the gift of salvation.

The Return to Nazareth, 2:39–40

Having presented Jesus to the Lord, Joseph and Mary return with Jesus to Nazareth. The account of Jesus' birth ends with a refrain that parallels the ending of the account of John the Baptist's birth in 1:80. There is, however, an important difference. While John developed in "body and spirit," Jesus not only grew in strength and wisdom, but also received the blessings of God (2:40). From his childhood Jesus was superior to the Baptist.

The Finding of Jesus in the Temple, 2:41–52

Our study of these twelve verses can provide new insight for us about the way in which biblical scholarship enriches our appreciation of the Scriptures. Since the Middle Ages popular Christian piety assumed that Luke began his account with the births of John and Jesus and then chronologically moved forward, tracing Jesus' life through boyhood, ministry, passion and resurrection. From this perspective it seemed that when Jesus was twelve, near the time of a young man's taking on some adult responsibilities as a "son of the covenant," Jesus joined Mary and Joseph on their annual journey to Jerusalem. When Mary and Joseph missed their son, they returned to the temple where they found Jesus in dialogue with the Jewish leaders. Readers took this incident as an account of an event in the "hidden life" of Jesus, not realizing that its deeper meaning could be had only by viewing the scene in the context of the rest of Luke's account.

We have seen the way in which Luke parallels the annunciations of John and Jesus and their birth stories. Now, with the introduction of the story of the twelve year old Jesus, that parallelism has lost some balance. Luke does not recount any event between John the Baptist's birth and his public appearance in the wilderness. The symmetry which Luke has so carefully developed earlier suggests that originally the infancy narrative ended with 2:40, so that the childhoods of John and Jesus remain parallel:

The child grew and developed in body and spirit (1:80).	The child grew and became strong; he was full of wisdom, and God's blessing was upon him (2:40).

It appears that the episode in 2:41–52 was added by Luke after he had completed his prologue. If this is so, why? Possibly Luke may have wanted to state even more clearly how his prologue functioned as a miniature portrait of the Gospel as a whole. Just as the shepherds symbolize the poor for whom Jesus has come, and just as the prophecies of Simeon and Anna pointed to Jesus' mission to save the Gentiles and set Israel free, the account of the finding of the twelve year old Jesus seems to foreshadow not only his ministry and death, but also his resurrection and ascension to the Father. The clues that lead to this interpretation are found in the text of the Gospel.

The journey to Jerusalem (2:41) prefigures the journey Jesus will resolutely make to Jerusalem at the end of his Galilean ministry (see 9:51). Mary and Joseph find Jesus with the Jewish leaders (2:46), amazing all who listen to his answers. So it will be throughout Jesus' teaching ministry. He will be a teacher, a wisdom figure, a prophet. When Mary and Joseph return to Jerusalem, they find Jesus in the temple "on the third day" (2:46). This anticipates the climax of the Gospel, in which the risen Jesus declares to his disciples that the Messiah had to rise from death on the third day (24:46).

It is noteworthy that Mary speaks for both herself and Joseph, pointing out their anxiety and asking Jesus for the reason why he has done what he did (2:48). If Mary is, according to Luke, the model disciple, then she represents the entire believing community. Perhaps her anxiety and her question speak for Luke's community of the 80s, a church anxiously asking "Where is Jesus?" or "Why isn't he with us now?" The answer Jesus gives to Mary may also be intended for the puzzled Christians in Luke's audience: "Didn't you know that I had to be in my Father's house?" (2:49). This answer conveys the same sense of necessity expressed in the statements of the risen Jesus at the end of the Gospel: "Was it not necessary for the Messiah to suffer . . . and then enter into his glory?" (24:26) To be in his Father's house can be seen as a reference to Jesus' ascension to his Father. The movement of Jesus to his Father summarizes Luke's account of the good news.

It is appropriate that Mary and Joseph are depicted as not understanding Jesus' answer (2:50), because the meaning of Jesus' relationship with his Father will only be clear in his death, resurrection and ascension. Luke's assertion in 2:50 is related to the amazement of all at the shepherds' message (2:18), the prophecy that a sword would pierce Mary's heart (2:35), and then the pondering and treasuring of "these things" in her heart (2:19, 51).

Week Two

In preparation for the public ministry of Jesus, Luke includes the historical setting, the preaching of John the Baptist, God's affirmation of Jesus after his baptism, Jesus' genealogy and the dramatization of his temptations in the wilderness. Luke deliberately downplays the person and ministry of John the Baptist. Thus Luke does not include the Baptist's declaration that the kingdom of God is at hand, but leaves this proclamation exclusively for Jesus (4:43). Luke describes the baptism of Jesus without a direct reference to John. By this means Luke establishes the importance of Jesus. The Baptist may have been the greatest prophet of Israel and the herald of the Lord, but he fades into the background as Jesus begins his public ministry in Galilee.

That ministry begins dramatically with Jesus' sermon in the synagogue at Nazareth. This is followed by acts of exorcism and healing. Jesus begins to call his disciples, enters into conflict with the religious leaders of Israel, and, after spending the night in prayer, chooses his twelve apostles.

DAILY STUDY ASSIGNMENTS: WEEK TWO

Day	Luke	Commentary
1	3:1–38	pp. 40–44
2	4:1–30	pp. 44–53
3	4:31–44	pp. 53–57
4	5:1–11	pp. 57–59
5	5:12–6:11	pp. 59–66

6 Review Luke 3:1–6:11 in light of the following questions and the guidance of the Holy Spirit.

7 Group meeting for sharing.

1. John the Baptist called for repentance/conversion. What might be some of the questions that could be raised by the inhabitants of your community if the Baptist were preaching in your city or neighborhood? What advice might he have for the ordinary citizen, the police, the media people, the politicians, the leaders in your parish, the members of your parish?

2. Is it "practical" to ask people to suspend their previous judgments long enough to rethink seriously long-held personal positions in light of God's priorities? What areas of your life would you not want to rethink? Why?

3. The American bishops have written two controversial pastoral letters, one dealing with the issues of war and peace, the other dealing with the American economic system. How might the preaching of John (3:7–14) and Jesus (4:18–21) be connected with the pastoral letters and rethinking one's priorities?

4. How could you personally extend the ministry of Jesus through the opportunities you have to serve others (in the home, family, parish, place of employment, neighborhood and nation)? Share some of these with your group.

5. Peter declared, "Leave me, Lord; I am a sinful man." Levi was a tax collector (commonly a dishonest profession in the time of Jesus). Since Jesus called them to be his followers, would Jesus' choice of Simon and Levi have an influence on the way you now perceive socially undesirable people? Should it have an influence?

The Preaching of John the Baptist, 3:1–20

The dramatic historical setting in which Luke presents the appearance of John the Baptist may have been the way he originally began his account of the good news prior to the addition of the infancy narrative. John's emphasis is on repentance and his manifest concern for the poor and the powerless serve as fitting introduction to the ministry of Jesus.

Historians date the fifteenth year of Tiberius' rule as 28 or 29 A.D. Luke situates John in the historical context of both the Roman empire and the Jewish people. These secular rulers are named beginning with the Roman emperor and concluding with the local leaders. After recognizing the contemporary religious leaders, Luke leads us to the climax of the introduction: "At that time the word of God came to John son of Zechariah in the desert" (3:2). Mention of the phrase "word of God" links John with the prophetic tradition, particularly with Jeremiah (Jer 1:5) who was also consecrated to God before birth. The mention of Zechariah also connects this section with the infancy narrative. Empowered by God's word, John travels the Jordan valley, proclaiming an ancient prophetic message: "Turn away from your sins and be baptized, and God will forgive your sins" (3:3). Mark's account of the good news applied the words of Isaiah to describe the role of the Baptist (Mk 1:2–3; Is 40:3). Luke follows Mark but extends the citation so that it concludes with the promise of salvation for all people: "All mankind will see God's salvation" (3:6). That salvation is not based on race or religion, even though one may already be a descendant of Abraham (3:7). God's salvation is universal, for both Jew and Gentile, but the condition for receiving this gift is a willingness to do what God asks.

The desert location of John's preaching would remind his audience of the fact that it was in the desert that God had entered into a covenant relationship with his people (see Ex 24:3–8). Since the covenant (found in the Torah, the first five books of the Bible) was the link between God and his people, the observance of the covenant became the heart of the prophetic tradition. But for several centuries no prophet had been sent to Israel. Now there was John. He called for people to go back to God by going beyond themselves in the reordering of their priorities so that they would put ultimate values before all others. As shall be seen, the theme of "turning from sin" is crucial in Luke's theology.

Some people in the Baptist's audience respond to his call for immediate and total conversion. They want to know how to turn from their sins in order to avoid the axe of God's wrath (3:9). The Baptist's answers (3:10–14) introduce key themes that appear throughout the Third Gospel. John instructs the ordinary people to share their extra food and clothing with those who are in desperate need (3:11). The tax collectors are told to act justly, rather than using the system to grow rich at the expense of others (3:13). The soldiers too are told to act justly, avoiding the practice of shakedowns and extortion (3:14).

Luke emphasizes that it is not the religious leaders who listen to John's message, but rather the religious outcasts. The common people, the tax collectors, the persons in the despised occupations, are the very ones who will soon be the focus of Jesus' ministry.

The Jewish people are so filled with messianic expectations that they begin to think of John as the one Israel awaits (3:15). John then distances himself from any claim to that title. He subordinates himself to Jesus by describing him as the one "who is greater than I" (3:16). The description of Jesus as the one who comes to baptize "with the Holy Spirit and fire" both looks ahead to Pentecost and characterizes Jesus as the ultimate judgment of God. While Jesus is compassionate and forgiving, he is also the one who makes demands on his followers. In a very real way Jesus is the crisis of a believer's life. In confronting Jesus, one must make a decision. In the Gospel any scene involving separation is a scene of judgment, and Jesus is the razor edge of separation:

> *He has his winnowing shovel with him to thresh out all the grain and will gather the wheat into his barn; but he will burn the chaff in a fire that never goes out (3:17).*

Note that judgment is twofold. On the one hand, judgment is destructive: the axe separates root from tree; the fire separates the metal from the slag; the fruitless tree and the chaff go into the fire. On the other hand, judgment is redemptive: the fruit-bearing tree is saved; the grain is gathered into the barn; the repentant sinners enter the kingdom of God.

After witnessing to Jesus, John has almost completed his part in the drama of salvation. Luke concludes John's public ministry by referring to his imprisonment by Herod. John will not be seen again. Shortly after his disciples come to Jesus (7:18ff), John the prophet will die a martyr's death.

The Baptism of Jesus, 3:21–22

Note how Luke reworks his Markan source in a way that downplays the baptism of Jesus by John:

Not long afterward Jesus came from Nazareth in the province of Galilee, and was baptized by John in the Jordan (Mk 1:9).

After all the people had been baptized, Jesus also was baptized (3:21).

In Luke's understanding, the importance of the event lies not so much in the baptism of Jesus as in a revelation by the Father and the Holy Spirit of Jesus' identity. Luke alone notes that the revelation took place while Jesus was at prayer (3:21).

The revelation seems to be for Jesus alone. For one steeped in the Hebrew Scriptures these words would have profound meaning. The Father's words, "You are my own dear Son. I am well pleased with you" (3:22), combine themes from Psalm 2 and the Book of Isaiah. Psalm 2 speaks of God's anointed king:

I will announce . . . what the Lord has declared. He said to me: "You are my son; today I have become your father. Ask, and I will give you all the nations; the whole earth will be yours" (Ps 2:7–8).

The citation from Isaiah describes the mission of Jesus and alludes to the kind of Messiah he will be:

The Lord says, "Here is my servant, whom I strengthen—the one I have chosen, with whom I am pleased. I have filled him with my spirit, and he will bring justice to every nation" (Is 42:1).

This quotation from Isaiah is of great importance, for it contains the key to the identity of Jesus the Messiah: Jesus is the suffering servant of God—the one with whom God is pleased (3:22). This can be said because the citation from Isaiah 42:1 is taken from the opening line of the first of four poems or hymns depicting the rejection and trial of a mysterious servant through whom God will save his people. These four servant hymns are contained in chapters 42 through 53 of Isaiah. It seems that these poems were largely ignored, the idea of redemption through suffering being as repugnant then as it is in our own day.

The Genealogy of Jesus, 3:23–38

At the baptism the Father spoke of Jesus as the Son (Ps 2:7) with whom he was pleased (Is 42:1). Luke now writes of Jesus' family lineage in a way that connects the baptismal revelation with Isaiah's theme of universality. Thus Luke traces the origins of Jesus back to Adam (3:38). While Matthew took the lineage of Jesus back to Abraham (Mt 1:1–2), Luke points out that Jesus is not only related to the Jewish people but also to the entire human family. The good news is that through Jesus salvation comes to everyone as Isaiah had foretold: "All mankind will see God's salvation" (Is 40:5; Lk 3:6).

The Temptations of Jesus, 4:1–13

Jewish people of Jesus' day had strong convictions about the reality of good and evil spirits. Among the evil spirits one of the most powerful was known as Satan or the devil. The devil was seen as one who placed obstacles in the path of God's people. This would happen in two basic ways: (1) inflicting people with physical or mental illness; (2) inciting people to rebel against God's purposes. The latter is seen as Satan's role in the account of the temptations of Jesus in the desert.

The call to be God's suffering servant, as revealed in the baptismal vision, must have seemed a terrifying mission for Jesus. He seeks a place to pray and prepare. Jesus had been filled with the Holy Spirit at his baptism. Now the Spirit leads him into the desert (4:1).

Mark recounts only that Jesus was tempted by Satan (Mk 1:13). Luke and Matthew, probably using a common source, record three temptations. Each temptation may be seen as an attempt to convince Jesus to abandon the role of the suffering servant for another kind of messianic mission. Thus this desert experience can be thought of as the crossroads of his life. Following the understanding of the temptations of Jesus as put forward in *A Commentary on the Gospel of Matthew*, it can be said that two roads spread out before Jesus. To the left is a broad and well traveled road that represents conformity to the popular messianic expectations of the Jewish people. They are looking for independence from the Romans, political power and prosperity. To travel this road would mean acceptance, acclaim and the guarantee of a certain kind of success. But, to the right, is hardly a road at all. Rocky and untraveled, this road represents the journeying of the suffering servant who seeks to do God's will come what may. To travel down this road is to confront people with a clash between common sense values and the values that demand a reversal of the usual human ways of thinking and perceiving. To journey this road entails probable rejection and disgrace.

In the first temptation it is suggested to Jesus that he take the road to the left, bringing the prosperous times symbolized by a new manna miracle that would make bread on the table as plentiful as rocks in the desert (4:3).

Remembering the word of God, Jesus cites the words of Deuteronomy that stress doing the will of God:

> *Remember how the Lord your God led you on this long journey through the desert these past forty years, sending hardships to test you, so that he might know what you intended to do and whether you would obey his commands. He made you go hungry, and then he gave you manna to eat. . . . He did this to teach you that man must not depend on bread alone to sustain, but on everything the Lord says (Dt 8:2–3).*

In Matthew's account (Mt 4:5–7) the second temptation suggests that Jesus perform a spectactular work in Jerusalem in order to gain the attention of the people. (In John 7:2–4 we may see the original context of this temptation.) Then, according to Matthew, the ultimate testing is Satan's offer of power and dominion over the kingdoms of the world (Mt 4:8–10). Luke, however, because he considers Jerusalem as the central stage for the drama of salvation, reordered the sequence of the second and third temptations in order to make Jerusalem the site of the third and final temptation. Thus the second temptation of Jesus according to Luke is the temptation to take dominion over the kingdoms of the world (4:5–7). The price to be paid is high: abandonment of the Father's will by submission to Satan (4:7). While this temptation seems outrageous, the fact is that it tells us much about the climate and times in which Jesus lived. Given the history of Israel, with such warrior leaders as Joshua, Gideon, King David, and the Maccabees, given the popular messianic expectations of the Jewish people, given the harsh Roman military occupation, and given the efforts of such nationalists as the zealots, it is possible to see how a charismatic leader could bring back the kind of independence and power Israel had under King David. Popular support, nationalism and the feeling that "God is on our side" could have given the right man an army of keenly disciplined, highly motivated patriots. It could have been a new era in Israel's secular history. In its center could have been the nationally acclaimed messiah, Jesus of Nazareth! Jesus again cited Deuteronomy:

> *Have reverence for the Lord your God, worship only him, and make your promises in his name alone. Do not worship other gods . . . (Dt 6:13–14).*

In the third temptation Jesus sees Jerusalem from the perspective of the high tower of the temple from which the priests call the people to prayer at the beginning of each day (4:9). A spectactular descent from this point would surely gain Jesus a large following as he fulfilled the passage in Psalm 91 which declares that God's angels will protect his servant. Jesus refuses, for the third time holding to his Father's will as the priority of his life:

> *Do not put the Lord your God to the test, as you did at Massah. Be sure that you obey all the laws that he has given you (Dt 6:16–17).*

Defeated, Satan withdraws (4:13). Jesus has chosen to do his Father's will. He accepts the call to be God's suffering servant. There, in the desert, with the help of the Spirit, Jesus has succeeded where Israel had failed. His forty days in the desert recall the forty years Moses had led the people. In the desert they had yielded to temptation, but Jesus has remained faithful. He is ready to begin his ministry.

REFLECTION. The recounting of these temptations tells us about the humanity of Jesus. Like us, he had the freedom to make choices. He was not a puppet, nor was his Father a puppeteer. At the beginning of his ministry Jesus struggled to make proper choices. It was a struggle because there was goodness in each one of the options he had before him. It would have been good to give people bread and prosperity. It would have been a worthy and patriotic deed to free Israel of the Roman colonizers. It would have been good to be recognized and acclaimed as a gifted leader whom God miraculously protected. None of these choices are inherently evil.

But there was a better choice: to love his people even more deeply by doing his Father's will as he perceived it. The Father invited Jesus to minister not by standing above the human condition but by becoming involved in the lives of people—our lives. Ours is a wounded humanity. So Jesus entered into our hurting situation with his whole person. That meant taking the risk of being rejected, wounded, and even destroyed. And that happened. Not only could Jesus rejoice with those who are grateful for the gift of life, he could also grieve with the grieving, hunger with the hungry, and feel the suffering of the poor. All of his experiences became the wellsprings of his understanding of the human condition. We can say that his Father asked him to be fully human, for only then is he able to be a model for all of us who share that same humanity. He showed us how the quest to do our Father's will in every circumstance enables us to recognize that in his will is our peace. Our own experiences of struggle and suffering can become sources of meaning and healing for others.

The Beginnings of the Galilean Ministry 4:14–44

OVERVIEW. In Luke's ordered account (1:3) the divisions of Jesus' ministry are clearly drawn. The first portion (4:14–9:50) speaks of Jesus preaching, healing and exorcising in Galilee; the middle tells of Jesus' journey to Jerusalem (9:51—19:27); the final section depicts Jesus' ministry in Jerusalem (19:28—24:53). When we look at how Luke uses the Gospel written by Mark, we see that Luke follows Mark with one major exception. Luke omits Mark's narration of Jesus' journeys into the Gentile areas of Tyre and Sidon (Mk 6:45–8:26). By doing this Luke shows a clear connection between Jesus' ministry in Galilee and his subsequent rejection in Jerusalem.

Jesus Begins His Ministry, 4:14–15

COMMENTARY. This short section sums up the initial stages of Jesus' ministry. Filled with the power of the Spirit, Jesus begins to preach in the synagogues of Galilee. People enthusiastically accept him. His reputation spreads throughout the area.

Jesus at Nazareth, 4:16–30

This section is found only in Luke. It is likely that these fifteen verses represent three different episodes in Jesus' ministry: the initial preaching of Jesus and its acceptance (4:18–22a); the people's demand for special signs and their willingness to place their trust in Jesus on the basis of his person and his message (4:22b–24); their rejection of Jesus in the attempt to put him to death (4:25–30). The third episode may well be Luke's theological explanation of the rejection of Jesus by Judaism and the origins of the call of the Gentiles to faith.

The events happening in the Nazareth synagogue are highly dramatic. As Jesus reads from the prophet Isaiah, events long ago foretold begin to happen. God's will to save his people begins to be realized in the presence and person of Jesus. At the very beginning of his work Jesus sounds the keynotes of his ministry: the preaching of the good news to the poor, the granting of liberty to captives, the bringing of new sight to the blind, and the setting free of the oppressed. All these are the signs of God's gracious mercy!

The synagogue service probably consisted of three parts: prayer, Scripture reading and teaching. Having been given the scroll of Isaiah by the synagogue assistant, Jesus seeks out the passage (Is 61:1-2) which declares God's promise to restore Israel through his anointed prophet. Upon that prophet God's Spirit will rest. Recall that Jesus is the one who had received the Spirit as he prayed after his baptism (3:22) That same Spirit of God had led Jesus into the desert (4:1) and was present to him as he preached throughout Galilee (4:14).

Jesus is sent, above all, to proclaim good news to the poor. In Luke "the poor" are those who recognize their dependence upon God for everything. He frequently uses those who have no material resources as models of this poverty, since their spiritual "empty-handedness" is not disguised by worldly possessions. In addition, the materially poor become instruments of God's saving work for the well-to-do. By extending mercy to the poor and by sharing the goods of this life with the have-nots of society, the believing community fashions a solidarity among all people.

The reference to the freeing of captives (4:18) appears

twice in the Book of Isaiah (Is 58:6–61:1). Note the context of Isaiah 58:6. Isaiah is telling the people of Israel that the Lord has indicted them for fasting without practicing justice. As we have seen with Jesus' citing of Deuteronomy during his temptations, when one line of the word of God is cited, the sentences preceding and following the specific quotation help us see the overall meaning more clearly:

> *The Lord says to them, "The truth is that at the same time you fast, you pursue your own interests and oppress your workers. . . . The kind of fasting I want is this: Remove the chains of oppression and the yoke of injustice and let the op-pressed go free. Share your food with the hungry and open your homes to the homeless poor. Give clothes to those who have nothing to wear, and do not refuse to help your own rel-atives. Then . . . your wounds will be quickly healed. I will always be with you to save you" (Is 58:3–8).*

Isaiah's admonitions to share food and clothing and to practice justice are also found on the lips of John the Baptist (3:11–14). The word used for proclaiming *liberty* to captives (4:18) is also used by Luke to denote the forgiveness of sins.

The announcement that "the time has come when the Lord will save his people" is a reference to the jubilee year spoken of in Leviticus 25:10. In the fiftieth year debts were forgiven and lands that had passed out of the original owner's hands would be restored as God justly redivided the earth among his chosen. Such was Isaiah's vision of the end-time, the period of God's powerful intervention in history on behalf of his people. With the crowd expectantly waiting, the eyes of all upon him, Jesus declares that the text of Isaiah is fulfilled now—in their very hearing (4:21)! The people's immediate response is one of amazement and admiration of Jesus (4:22a).

Verses 22b–24 seem to speak of a subsequent visit to

Nazareth. At this point the townspeople begin to resist Jesus' teaching because he lacks special status. It is likely that Luke is combining several events into this episode. The people of Nazareth have heard of Jesus' miraculous healings in neighboring Capernaum and demand to see similar works in their midst. Yet they lack the necessary faith, seeing in Jesus only "the son of Joseph." Using folk wisdom (4:23–24) Jesus expresses their reluctance to receive him as one chosen by God.

Verses 25 through 30 could summarize a third visit to Nazareth. In these verses Luke seems to be offering his theological explanation of the rejection of Jesus by the majority of the Jewish people and the subsequent acceptance of Jesus by the Gentiles. The gist of Jesus' references to Elijah and Elisha is that both of these Israelite prophets ministered to Gentile persons. Even though Israel appeared to be more worthy in view of the fact that they were God's chosen people, God had elected Elijah to aid a Gentile widow in Sidon (1 Kgs 17:7–24). In his second example, Jesus refers to the fact that although there were many Jewish lepers in the time of Elisha, it was the Gentile Naaman who was cured (2 Kgs 5:1–24).

The angry response to Jesus (4:28) is similar to Luke's description of the violent rejection of Stephen by the Jewish people in Acts 7:58. What happens first with Jesus will happen again in the development of the church. The taking of Jesus out of town and to the top of a nearby cliff (4:29) anticipates his crucifixion. Some scholars see a reference to the resurrection in the description of Jesus walking through the hostile crowd. The escape of Jesus through the mob is not necessarily miraculous. At the crucial moment Jesus could have boldly faced his opposition. No one dared to take the initiative of hurling him off the cliff, and thus he walked through their midst (4:30).

REFLECTION. Jesus declared that he had come to proclaim the Gospel to the poor, bring sight to the blind, set the captives free and announce God's salvation. Should it be a surprising thought that we, the Church, are called to continue the mission of Jesus in word and deed? Since we are the living presence of Jesus in the world now, our basic task is more "this-worldly" than "other-worldly." As the *Constitution on the Church in the Modern World* points out, while earthly progress cannot be identified with the growth of Christ's kingdom, "to the extent that earthly progress can contribute to the better ordering of human society, it is of vital concern to the kingdom of God" (art. 39). We who are called to be Jesus' disciples have the task of transforming society so that human life is characterized more by peace than by war, more by hope than by an acceptance of the status quo, more by cooperation than by individualistic competition, and more by justice than by the marginalizing of the weak and poor.

A Day at Capernaum, 4:31–44

COMMENTARY. In verses 31 through 44, Luke follows Mark's depiction of a typical day in the life of Jesus—a day spent in teaching, exorcising and healing. While Jesus is teaching in the synagogue, a man "who had the spirit of an evil demon in him" (4:33) confronts the one who has "the power of the Holy Spirit with him" (4:14). By naming Jesus and describing him as "God's holy messenger," the evil spirit may have been trying to exercise some power over him. The attempt fails as Jesus commands the spirit to be silent. Luke notes that the spirit departed without doing the man any harm. This is the first act of power Jesus performs in Luke's Gospel account, the healing of a person held captive by the power of evil.

The amazed response of the crowd centers on the "words" of Jesus (4:36). Here Luke uses "words" in the technical sense of Christian preaching. Thus the exorcism is depicted as a teaching, and the reputation of Jesus spreads through the countryside. In a culture with a world view quite different from ours, the power of Jesus is very convincingly portrayed.

In the next scene Jesus is presented as a healer of the sick and diseased (4:38–41). In Mark's account Jesus calls four fishermen to be his disciples, and then cures Simon's mother-in-law (Mk 1:16–31). Luke restructures the chronology of Mark by putting the cure before the calling. Perhaps this is done to provide a rationale for why the four men answer Jesus' call to discipleship in the following episode. It could have happened that Jesus' disciples first believed in him because of the acts of power he performed.

After sunset, that is, at the end of the sabbath day of rest, Jesus does many works of healing and exorcising. Jesus silences the demons not only because they have an inadequate understanding of his messiahship, but also because belief for Luke is more than acknowledgement that Jesus is the Messiah. To believe in Jesus is to follow him. While the demonic forces can mimic the words of faith, they cannot become Jesus' disciples. Thus they are silenced.

Jesus Preaches the Kingdom of God, 4:42–44

In response to the effort of the people of Capernaum's to keep him from leaving, Jesus tells them he must preach the good news of the kingdom of God elsewhere. There is an urgency here, a necessity. Jesus must do what he is sent to do. Later Luke will record Jesus' words about the necessity of his suffering and dying. In 4:43 we find the first mention of the kingdom of God by Jesus in Luke's account. One way to appreciate Jesus' preaching of the kingdom is to see its meaning in comparison and contrast with the preaching of John the Baptist (3:7–17). John warned about the imminent judgment of God upon a sinful people. The end-time was at hand.

Jesus is different. He sees his mission in terms of a hopeful expectation of the approaching "reign" or "rule" of God. The kingdom of God is coming and with his rule comes salvation for his people (4:18–19). That salvation is now being manifested in terms of God's activity in Jesus. We catch a glimpse of God's coming kingdom in the two cures worked by Jesus—the healing of the possessed man and of Peter's mother-in-law (4:31–39). God's rule over the world shall bring peace, health and wholeness to all peoples.

REFLECTIONS. Regarding 4:33–35, people sometimes find themselves asking, "Did Jesus really carry on a conversation with demonic forces inside the sick (possessed) man?" Rather than separate the Gospel into parts that "really happened" and parts that "might not have really happened," it is best to see what Luke is trying to communicate. To do this it is necessary to understand the first century perspective. The people living then made a distinction between the demon and the devil. The demon was seen as connected with anything that was a problem of a mysterious or unexplainable nature. Epilepsy and mental illness were such problems. The people living then attributed such problems to demons. Demons were thought of as inhabiting a person and thereby working from within to cause the strange behavior manifested by that person. Jesus cured people of some inexplicable behaviors. The people referred to Jesus' cures in terms of his casting out evil demons.

A devil was perceived by first century people as a spirit that worked on people from the outside; it did not inhabit or possess a person. The devil was viewed as a stumbling block which must be resisted with one's inner strength. Hence the temptations that suggested to Jesus that he turn aside from doing God's will are attributed to the devil (4:2–13).

How are we, twentieth century Christians living in a scientific age and a vastly different world view, to perceive these narrations of encounters with demons and devils? In answer to this question, it can be said that we can perceive both the first century and the twentieth century world views with certain reservations. Demons were acceptable explanations of disorders that first century people could not explain in any other way. Germs, damaged genes and chemical imbalances are acceptable explanations of human disorders in our time. Yet the twentieth century world view has a serious weakness. The scientific view leaves little room for mystery; it seems able to provide answers for everything. The first century perspective saw the world as the arena of salvation, with God in power and evil spirits resisting that power. Perhaps it is better to live with some ambiguity, knowing that our human and theological knowledge will continue to develop indefinitely.

Having made these observations about the world views of first and twentieth century persons, let us return to the Gospel account. There is a double aspect to Jesus' preaching of God's kingdom. On the one hand, God already exercises his saving power through Jesus' cures and exorcisms. On the other hand, God's kingdom is not completely present. People continue to harm their neighbors and refuse to love God. Thus God's complete reign is related to the final destiny of the world. By proclaiming the beginning of the coming kingdom of God, Jesus declares that humanity has a meaningful future. We are to live in hope because God will be faithful to his promises.

In his encyclical letter, *On Evangelization in the Modern World,* Pope Paul VI brought together the world views of the first and the twentieth century by connecting Jesus' proclamation of God's kingdom with the contemporary mission of the Church. The mission of Jesus and the mission of today's Church is described as the "liberation from everything that oppresses humankind . . . above all, liberation from sin and the evil one." Thus, in the contemporary Church it is not an acceptable theory that people in the time of Christ "invented" demons because they knew of no other way to explain certain happenings.

Jesus Calls the First Disciples, 5:1–11

OVERVIEW. Luke's account of the call of Simon Peter is quite different from those found in Mark and Matthew, who give us the impression that Jesus came, called Simon, Andrew, James and John, and led them away as his disciples. Luke might have composed his version from several different sources, or he might have received a tradition in which several stories had been blended together.

In Luke's telling we first learn something about the nature of Jesus' mission. He appeared in the synagogue at Nazareth and declared that he had come to fulfill what God had promised through the prophet Isaiah (4:18–21). Then Jesus provided a living example of prophecy fulfilled. He freed a man from demonic captivity, healed the sick and preached the good news. While Mark gives the impression that Peter never saw Jesus until the moment he was called

(Mk 1:16–20), Luke lets us know that Peter and the others witnessed the deeds and teaching of Jesus prior to their being invited to discipleship.

COMMENTARY. Luke sets the scene on the shore of Lake Gennesaret (the Sea of Galilee). It is morning and many people are listening to Jesus' preaching. To be better heard, Jesus asked Simon for the use of his boat as a speaker's platform. When Jesus finished speaking, he asked Simon to prepare for a catch in the deep water. Simon objects on the basis of his fisherman's experience—the night had proved fruitless and morning was not the time for netting fish. Nevertheless, on the basis of Jesus' authority, that is, on the strength of Jesus' word (5:5), Simon reluctantly tries again. To his astonishment, Simon nets so many fish that he needs help from the other boat. The catch is a sign that stirs up in Simon amazement and a religious fear because he knows he is in the presence of divine power. Before this moment Simon had referred to Jesus as "Master"; now Simon acknowledges his sinfulness and addresses Jesus by the divine title, "Lord" (5:5).

Jesus responds to Simon by commissioning him for a new calling: "From now on you will be catching men" (5:10). Having known Jesus as a healer and teacher, having seen his power, and having been called to assist Jesus in his mission, Simon Peter, James and John respond. They leave their boats and possessions in order to follow Jesus as his disciples (5:11).

REFLECTION. We who are called to be disciples of Jesus in virtue of our baptism and confirmation can find much to meditate upon in this episode. At different times in our lives it may seem that we do much work yet "catch nothing." At times such as these, the words of Jesus give us encouragement. Even though we are sinners, we can go out into the deep and be confident that with his presence we will bring in the achievements that God wills for us.

Bringing another perspective to bear on this episode we can ask: What does it mean to be fishing for people? Netting or catching fish does not seem to do anything helpful for the fish. Taken out of their environment, they die. What's the point of catching people, of taking people out of the sea? The answer is seen in light of the Jewish understanding of the sea and its symbolism. The Jews feared the sea, for it was a place of uncontrolled, destructive power. To journey out on the Mediterranean by boat was a terrifying venture. The sea symbolized chaos (Gen 1:1), and in it dwelt the Leviathan, the great monster of primeval destruction (Job 3:8). The sea held such terror for the people that the author of the Book of Revelation offered a vision of a new heaven and a new earth in which "there was no longer any sea" (Rev 21:1, JB). With this background in mind we see the depth of meaning in Jesus' calling Simon to share in his mission of pulling people out of the sea. To catch people is to become a co-laborer with Jesus in the great work of salvation.

Jesus Cleanses a Leper, 5:12–16

COMMENTARY. At this point Luke returns to his Markan source (cf. Mk 1:40ff). The leper, a social and religious outcast, requests of Jesus not a cure but to be cleansed. While being made clean implies a cure, his urgent pleading seems to reflect his deep loneliness more than physical suffering. The law (Lv 13:45–46) demanded that those who were unclean live outside the camp—away from society. The average person of Jesus' day made every effort to avoid those afflicted with leprosy. Normal human revulsion at horrible disfigurement could be freely expressed toward lepers. Jesus not only avoids shunning the leper, he reaches out to bridge the gulf which separated the leper from "clean" society. By his emphatic words, "I do want to" (make you clean), Jesus announces his urgent desire to bring this afflicted son of Abraham into the blessings of the covenant: health and life in community. For many centuries the Church has seen this beautiful encounter of Jesus and the leper as a parable of salvation. Each of us, in our own kind of affliction, uncleanness, or misery, is touched by Jesus and assured of his commitment to our wholeness.

Obedient to the Mosaic law, Jesus instructs the cleansed man to follow the prescriptions of the law. Luke softens Mark's account which holds the man blameworthy for not following Jesus' request for silence (Mk 1:45). Luke, wanting to stress Jesus' prayerful relationship with his Father as the source of his power to heal and preach, notes that Jesus retires to the lonely places in order to pray (5:16).

Jesus Heals a Paralyzed Man, 5:17–26

At this point Luke begins to narrate a series of incidents that illustrate the deepening conflict that developed between Jesus and his opponents. In this episode (5:17–26) the teachers of the law (scribes) and the Pharisees object to Jesus' declaring that a person's sins are forgiven. The same opponents then object to Jesus' eating with tax collectors and outcasts (5:27–32). Next Jesus' disciples are criticized for their lack of fasting (5:33–39). Pharisees then accuse the disciples of working (harvesting grain) on the sabbath (6:1–5). Finally, on another sabbath, some scribes and Pharisees try to catch Jesus in the act of breaking the sabbath (6:6–10). At the end of this series of conflict stories Luke notes that the enemies of Jesus were discussing what they "could do to Jesus" (6:11).

In this account of Jesus' healing a paralyzed man lowered through the roof, Luke follows Mark except for the introduction in 5:17. Here Luke notes that Pharisees and teachers of the law had come from all the towns of Galilee and Judea. It is unlikely that in the original setting of Jesus' early ministry there was such a universal Jewish following. Perhaps Luke is expressing what happened later when the early missionaries did spread the Gospel of Jesus crucified and risen to every town in Judea and Galilee.

At issue here is Jesus' authority to declare that a person's sins are forgiven (5:21). Jesus then heals the man, thereby indicating that both the healing of sickness and the forgiveness of sins are signs of the Messiah's mission to restore all things. The man left praising God and all those present did the same, recognizing the "marvelous things we have seen today" (5:26).

Jesus Calls Levi, the Tax Collector, 5:27–32

In this call of another disciple we begin to see more clearly the kind of people Jesus cared about. In all three Synoptic accounts the call of Levi (or Matthew according to Mt 9:9) appropriately follows the account of Jesus' forgiving and then healing the paralyzed man. Thus Levi's call becomes an illustration of the calling of sinners and of the basic meaning of Jesus' ministry.

Levi responds to Jesus' invitation by leaving his post, asking Jesus to come for dinner, and inviting his friends to the feast. His friends would be tax collectors and others whom the Pharisees and teachers of the law classed as outcasts (5:30). The Pharisees regarded those who did not keep the law in its entirety as sinners; they were relegated to the outskirts of the Jewish community. Tax collectors especially were looked upon with great disfavor by pious Jews, because their occupation involved them in activities that broke the laws regarding the sabbath and ritual purity. They were also considered as oppressors and traitors to their own people, because they collaborated with the foreign power. It is likely that Levi (Matthew) did not work for the Romans but for Herod Antipas.

That Jesus ate with tax collectors and outcasts/sinners is most significant. In his society eating with persons was an act of acceptance, a being with others in community. The Pharisees and their scribes were scandalized at Jesus' going into a home where the dietary laws were not likely to be observed and so they challenged Jesus about his doing so.

Jesus' answer indicates that he was less concerned about religious propriety than about the people's relationship with God: "People who are well do not need a doctor, but only those who are sick" (5:31). Jesus eats with sinners because his mission is to bring the alienated members of God's people back into their rightful relationship with his Father. Jesus' eating with tax collectors and outcasts is a concrete illustration of what he preaches. His table fellowship reflects his own attitude about the relationship of God and people. Jesus has come to liberate persons from the restrictive image of God that was often put forward by the religious leaders of Israel.

In Mark's account, which Luke is following, Jesus says, "I have not come to call respectable people, but outcasts" (Mk 2:17). Luke modifies this statement to read, "I have not come to call respectable people to *repent*, but the outcasts" (5:32). By eating with sinners Jesus is actually inviting them to change and join him in his concern for living according to his Father's will.

We may see this passage as one of the basic aspects of the Church's mission: to continue the ministry of Jesus by ministering to those who are most in need of God's merciful forgiveness.

The Question About Fasting, 5:33–39

Matthew, Mark and Luke all place the questions about fasting after the controversy about Jesus' eating with sinners. Both the Pharisees and the followers of the Baptist placed a strong emphasis on the practice of fasting. By referring to the joy of the guests in the presence of the bridegroom, Jesus is asserting that his message and his presence have a joyful aspect that deserves recognition. His being taken away (5:35) is a reference to his death. This verse may have been added by the early community as a justification of the practice of fasting on the part of the followers of Jesus.

Three independent sayings regarding clothes, wineskins and the preference for old wine are added to the discussion of fasting. These three sayings are linked more by an association of words and ideas than they are by logical sequence. The "parable" Jesus tells indicates that it is nonsense to ruin a new garment to obtain a patch for an old one (5:36). This saying of Jesus may reflect the situation of the Church in the latter half of the first century, a time when the followers of Jesus were struggling with the challenge of proclaiming the Gospel to the whole world while some members wanted to hold on to the old ways of Judaism. The third saying, found only in Luke, indicates that a person with a bias for the old wine, that is, deeply committed to the accustomed Jewish way of living and believing, will not want to taste the new wine of the Gospel (5:39).

Disputes over the Interpretation of the Sabbath Law, 6:1–11

OVERVIEW. The Second Vatican Council's *Dogmatic Constitution on Divine Revelation* points out that "those who seek out the intentions of the sacred writers must . . . have regard for 'literary forms' " (art. 12). One such "literary form" is the conflict story, two of which are found in 6:1–11. "Form criticism" is a branch of literary science that singles out the different literary forms used by an author in a particular work, and then seeks to determine the reasons why and in what circumstances these stories were remembered and handed on. The following incidents seem to have been passed on in the Church because the disciples of the risen Jesus were involved in similar conflicts, for example, the proper ways to observe the law, how much involvement there should be with sinners/outcasts, etc. Form criticism shows that the Gospel is made up of material that had circulated in oral form long before it was written down. These stories were retold to meet the needs of the community's members, while being based on incidents in the life of Jesus.

COMMENTARY. To understand more fully these conflict stories, let us look first at the wider historical context. Decades before Jesus was born, the followers of two famous rabbis, Shammai and Hillel, were vigorously debating about different interpretations of the law. The followers of Shammai called for a strict interpretation of the various aspects of the Mosaic law. The school of Rabbi Hillel favored a more lenient perspective, one that made allowances for both unexpected circumstances as well as the changing needs of human living. Opinion was divided among the Pharisees on the question of the lawfulness of picking ears of corn to eat on the sabbath. The strict interpreters, the school of Shammai, held this action to be contrary to the sabbath law. This is the group within the Pharisaic movement that would have reproached the disciples of Jesus for "doing what our Law says you cannot do on the Sabbath" (6:2).

Luke abbreviates Mark's account of this incident (Mk 2:23–28) as he cites Jesus' scriptural example of an incident when David broke the law for the sake of feeding his hungry followers. Luke closes his account of this incident with Jesus' declaration, "The Son of Man is Lord of the Sabbath" (6:5). This would have important implications for Luke's Gentile audience. Since Jesus is the exalted Lord, he is ruler of the sabbath. His followers need not adhere to the ritual laws of Judaism.

The second controversy involves the dispute about the man with the crippled hand (6:6–11). Luke tells us that some teachers of the law and Pharisees are looking for reasons to undermine Jesus' reputation. It appears that Jesus' teaching about God's concern for the sinners and the nobodies and his interpretation of the law has upset the established religious leaders. They plan to destroy Jesus' credibility by exposing him as one who breaks God's law. Thus they watch him to see if he would cure on the sabbath, for this would amount to performing a forbidden work. Realizing what they were looking for, Jesus confronted them with a different kind of question. Jesus pointed out that the issue was not the lawfulness of curing on the sabbath, but whether the law allows a person to help or harm a person on the sabbath (6:9). It is a fine point of rabbinic argument that Jesus is bringing before the audience in the synagogue. In front of Jesus stands a man with a crippled hand. Everyone can see him. If Jesus has the ability to cure this crippled man, then not to do so would be the equivalent of harming him, that is, leaving him crippled. Since the law does not demand harming anyone, Jesus implies that the law calls for him to cure this man, that is, to help him. That is what Jesus does, much to the chagrin of the Pharisees and scribes. Having lost the confrontation, they react with desperate perplexity because Jesus is threatening their position as authorities in the interpretation of the law (6:11).

Week Three

After spending the night in prayer, Jesus chooses the twelve apostles (6:12–16) and begins teaching a large crowd of people. The "Sermon on the Plain" (6:17–49) contains four beatitudes and four woes that turn human expectations upside down. The rich, the satisfied and the successful are the ones to be pitied, for they do not recognize their need for God's saving power; the poor, the hungry and the sorrowing are the truly blessed.

Jesus travels about Galilee, healing and teaching. He raises a widow's only son from the dead (7:11–17) and replies to the question asked by John the Baptist: "Are you the one . . . or should we expect someone else?" (7:20).

At the home of Simon the Pharisee Jesus declares that the love of a repentant woman has brought her God's forgiveness (7:36–50). Luke then provides us with a glimpse of the attitude Jesus showed toward women in 8:1-3. The parable of the sower has applications for the early Christian communities as well as connections with Mary as the model disciple (8:4–14; 19–21). This week's study concludes with Jesus' exorcising a demon-possessed man, healing a woman who had been suffering for twelve years and raising the daughter of Jairus (8:26–56).

DAILY STUDY ASSIGNMENTS: WEEK THREE

Day	Luke	Commentary
1	6:12–26	pp. 70–74
2	6:27–49	pp. 74–77
3	7:1–35	pp. 78–81
4	7:36–50	pp. 81–84
5	8:1–56	pp. 84–94

6 Review Luke 6:12—8:56 in light of the reflection questions.

7 Group meets for study and prayer.

1. Luke holds up Jesus as a model for his disciples. Thus Jesus prays before the important moments of his life. In 6:12–13 Jesus prays before he chooses the twelve apostles. Why is this action so important?

2. The "beatitudes" are addressed to the disciples (6:20). The "woes" may be addressed also to the disciples, or to the great crowd (6:17), or both. What are some ways that we Catholic Christians can creatively apply the beatitudes and woes to our own lives? Keep in mind that nowadays prophetic voices are calling for a "preferential option for the poor." Perhaps living in the spirit of Jesus' beatitudes will enable us to find solidarity with the poor. Can we walk with the poor in the sense that when we do hear their voices, we hear their words coming up to us not from below but from alongside?

3. John the Baptist expected a "fire-and-brimstone" Messiah (3:17). At the same time he was able to discern that Jesus, even though he did not meet his expectations,

might be the one Israel awaited (7:20). Jesus tells the delegation sent by John to consider his healing deeds and compassionate preaching, inviting John to believe in him. Do you think each of us would do well to be ready to revise our own perceptions of Jesus? Should we be ready to develop our understanding of Jesus? How can this study of the Gospel answer these questions?

4. Jesus' openness toward women went against the prevailing subordination of women that was found in first century Israel. Unfortunately, the Church as a community later accepted the cultural views of women's inferiority to men. A new consciousness is developing and the Church is rediscovering Jesus' attitude. Mention some of the ways this new awareness can lovingly introduce changes in the home, the place of work, the parish.

The Call of the Twelve, 6:12–16

COMMENTARY. Luke alone tells us that Jesus spent the night in prayerful communion with his Father prior to choosing twelve from among his disciples. According to Mark, Jesus chose the twelve and then said, "I have chosen you to be with me. . . . I will also send you out to preach and . . . to drive out demons" (Mk 3:14–15). Luke omits the reference to their work, thus stressing the fact that Jesus named them apostles. In this way Luke affirms that the most important role of the apostles is their official position in the early Church: they represent the twelve tribes of Israel.

The apostles are also key persons in the continuation of Jesus' ministry. In Galilee Jesus is beginning the process of establishing authentic witnesses. Looking back to the beginning of this account, recall that Luke declared that he was ordering the story of Jesus so that the people of his day could "learn how well founded the teaching is that you have received" (see 1:1–4). In Luke's second volume he will develop the role of the apostles as witnesses. Thus, immediately before his ascension Jesus tells his apostles, "You will be witnesses for me in Jerusalem, in all of Judea and Samaria, and to the ends of the earth" (Acts 1:8).

The early believers saw in the twelve apostles the renewal and continuation of Israel. Since the symbolic function of the twelve was of greater importance, much about the individual histories of the twelve has been forgotten. However, the early community thought it important to pass on the memory that one member of Jesus' band was called "the Patriot" (6:15), i.e., a zealot, one of those who were seeking the overthrow of Roman rule. Another member of the group will become "the traitor."

REFLECTION. One of Luke's main concerns is to show by Jesus' example how prayer is the foundation of Jesus' ministry. Luke wants us to see that the actions of Jesus flow out of his prayerful relationship with his Father. After Jesus was baptized, while in prayerful union with his Father, Jesus received a revelation in the form of symbol (the Holy Spirit "in bodily form like a dove") and prophetic affirmation (3:22). The power of this prayerful union with his Father enabled Jesus to resist temptation (4:1–13), choose his apostles (6:12), teach his disciples to pray (11:2), remain faithful to his Father's will in the face of overwhelming fear (22:41) and, finally, entrust himself to his Father even in death itself (23:46).

Summary of Jesus' Ministry, 6:17–19

COMMENTARY. Luke records the initial success of Jesus. Everywhere Jesus went he proclaimed that God's love was universal—no one was excluded. No one was unworthy of his Father's love; one's social or religious status was not an obstacle as long as one was willing to turn back to God. Jesus enabled the outcasts, the poor and the sick to recognize their dignity as persons loved by God. As a result, a great crowd from Jerusalem to the coastal cities gathers around Jesus. People are eager to be close to Jesus, to touch him. All who draw near are healed and set free. Luke places this beautiful summary of Jesus' ministry and power immediately before a challenging sermon.

The Beatitudes:
The Sermon on the Plains Begins, 6:20–26

OVERVIEW. Having come down from the hill where he had chosen his apostles, Jesus stands on "a level place" (6:17). In 6:20 we find the beginning of a long discourse by Jesus. In Matthew's account Jesus speaks from a mountainside because, writing primarily for Jewish Christians, Matthew wants to link Moses and his reception of the law on Mount Sinai with Jesus, the new Moses. In Matthew 5:3–12 there are eight beatitudes addressed to all present, while a ninth is addressed to the disciples. In Luke there are only four beatitudes. Luke parallels them with four "woes" (6:24–26), which reverse the human condition of the preceding verses.

We may consider this "Sermon on the Plain" (6:20–49) as a summary of the principles of the kingdom of God, a description of what it means to be a disciple of Jesus. We cannot avoid the challenge of this teaching by thinking of it as intended only for the original disciples; nor is this teaching meant only for a special group in the Church such as the clergy or those religious in vows. The beatitudes in particular are addressed to all of us, for they are an urgent invitation to seek out the will of God.

COMMENTARY. The beatitudes and woes have been subject to a number of interpretations. Those who favor the status quo have sometimes used these words of Jesus to keep the poor and oppressed content with their lot in life. Others have used the woes to berate the well-to-do and stir up discontent among the have-nots.

It is important to recognize that Jesus speaks in these verses (and in the entire sermon) from the perspective of the end of time. In the ministry of Jesus the end time has already begun. The poor, the hungry, the sorrowing, the rejected are those who are ready to welcome Jesus into their lives. Conversely, the rich, the full, and the successful have no room for the Lord's anointed. They sense no need of God's saving power.

The beatitudes and woes describe two conditions. There are those who constantly strain forward, looking for God's powerful intervention, longing for salvation. Before Jesus came these people savored the promises of God's saving work in the Hebrew Scriptures. (Read again Is 61:1–3, along with Is 25:6–9.) In his inaugural sermon Jesus announces that he has come to fulfill those promises (4:18–19). Ardently awaiting God's salvation, those who have nothing discover that salvation in Jesus. Through their faith in him, the promises of the end time are already fulfilled, although only partially in this life. This situation is "happy" because they have chosen to center their lives around that which is truly important.

Conversely, there are those whose lives are easy and full now. They have no felt need to depend on God, no real desire to long for his gifts. Thus they do not recognize in Jesus the in-breaking of God's kingdom. Preoccupied with the things of this world, they do not realize that the end time has already begun in the ministry of Jesus, reversing normal human values and attitudes. Their situation is "terrible" (6:24–26) because they have mistaken what is truly important in human life. When the new age arrives in its fullness, they will discover that the things in which they have invested their lives are worthless.

The beatitudes and woes are not blessings and curses but descriptions of opposing human conditions. Jesus acknowledges the blessed condition of those who are free enough to respond to God's saving deed. At the same time he declares the terrible peril of those whose "riches" blind them to their need for God.

REFLECTION. The beatitudes (6:20–23) and the woes (6:24–26) should be seen in tandem; they balance one another. The poor are declared happy because God's reign has graciously chosen them. The woes are not so much a condemnation of the rich as they are an invitation to repent, an opportunity to turn away from the kind of living that finds value only in possessions. Even though judgment may be imminent, the rich are urgently invited to reverse their priorities, thereby undoing the results of the neglect of their relationship with God and neighbor.

Why does Jesus teach that the poor, the hungry and the sorrowful are blessed? Why are the rich and the full pitied? The answer may lie in the effect that wealth has upon a person. Such a person is usually in a position of power. Other persons make their living by doing the bidding of the rich and powerful. The rich are usually able to have their own way. They feel that they have created their success. Accordingly, the rich are often unsympathetic to the poor, attributing their poverty to laziness, ignorance and lack of ambition. For such reasons and more, it is difficult for the rich person to relate to God in a right way. The rich have little inclination to perceive themselves as being dependent upon God, or in need of God's mercy. Pleased with their status in life, they give little thought to conversion.

The Love of Enemies, 6:27–36

COMMENTARY. In these ten verses Luke gathers sayings that speak of the kind of love that is most characteristic of the disciples of Jesus. Doing good to one's enemies, receiving a blow on the cheek and then offering one's other cheek (6:28–29) have been differently interpreted through the centuries. It may be said that Jesus is advocating non-retaliation more than he is advocating a posture of defense-lessness. The idea of refraining from retaliation when injured needs to be seen in the broader context of loving one's enemies, as well as in the wider context of Jesus' teaching on forgiveness as is found in the Lord's Prayer: "Forgive us our sins, for we forgive everyone who does us wrong" (11:4).

Retaliation, which is the return of evil for evil, would tend to negate a person's commitment to Jesus. An ethic of non-retaliation, that is, a refraining from returning harm for harm, would also be appropriate for a Church often subject to religious and social persecution. The teaching of Jesus deals basically with relationships that are interpersonal, not those on a worldwide scale. Thus, absolute pacifism was not an issue at the time Luke wrote this Gospel account. However, these words of Jesus did form the basis of the Christian pacifism of the first three centuries. Moreover, these words of Jesus challenge us, his twentieth century disciples, to take a fresh look at the use of force to defend ourselves and our possessions.

The teaching on lending and expecting nothing back (6:30, 35) seems to have a deeper meaning than giving away one's possessions. The basic idea is that we should help other people without expecting to be repaid. In this way the disciple imitates God's generosity.

In 6:31 we find what has been named "the golden rule." In Jewish tradition this rule was known in a negative form: "What is hateful to you, do not do to your fellow-creature." Jesus adapts this traditional Jewish wisdom for his disciples. The key to his vision, already spelled out in

6:32–35, is positive, loving service of others. If this love is restricted only to friends and neighbors, then the disciples of Jesus are not different than anyone else (6:32–34). Proof that one is a disciple of Jesus is love even of one's enemies, after the example of the heavenly Father (6:35).

It is noteworthy to see how both Luke and Matthew adapted the collection of the sayings of Jesus (the Q source) to their particular audiences. In Matthew we read, "You must be perfect just as your heavenly Father is perfect" (Mt 5:48). For Matthew's Jewish Christian audience the ideal was the perfect keeping of God's will (Mt 5:20–47). In Luke we read, "Be compassionate as your Father is compassionate" (6:36). For Luke's Gentile Christians the compassion of God was the ideal norm for their generosity, service, and forgiveness. The parable of the loving Father, which is found only in Luke's account, well serves as an apt illustration of the compassion of God (15:11–32).

Judging Others, 6:37–42

Verses 37–38, 41–42 have their source in common Jewish wisdom. Their form is rabbinic: instruction and illustration. Jewish tradition urged lenient judgment of others, in the spirit of our own proverbial saying, "Don't judge another until you've walked a mile in his shoes." As he often does, Jesus adds a radical dimension to a common saying by declaring that one should not judge another at all!

Verses 39–40 provide another example of the freedom used by the Gospel writers. In Matthew the reference to the blind leading the blind is a critique of the scribes and Pharisees. Luke takes these same words and turns them into an exhortation to be an informed disciple, a pupil who becomes like his teacher.

A Tree and Its Fruit, 6:43-45

Luke gives us the words of Jesus in a form that describes how one's deeds reflect the goodness that is at the core of a truly religious person. The disciple's behavior emerges from the center of his or her being. If there is true conversion to the person and values of Jesus, then the life of the disciple will manifest that. In this sense we might say that the "good person who brings good out of the treasure of good things in his heart" (6:45) is self-centered in a good way. The one who "brings bad out of his treasure of bad things" is not truly self-centered but rather self-indulgent.

The Two House Builders, 6:46-49

Luke brings the Great Sermon to a close by stressing how crucial it is to do and to live the teachings of Jesus. In Luke 6:46-47 the contrast is not between those who hear Jesus' word and those who refuse to hear it, but between those who listen and obey and those who listen and do not put that word into practice. The one who hears and practices the teaching of Jesus is likened to a builder who dug deep so that he could lay his foundation on rock. The one who hears and does not live out the teaching has no foundation set on rock. Outwardly the two houses may look the same, but when the river floods—a symbol for the judgment of God—the quality of each house's foundation will be revealed. Thus durability or collapse at the judgment depends on where a disciple builds his house. We are often tempted to build our lives on the surface of things, but the only adequate site on which to build our lives is the bedrock of loving and faithful obedience to Jesus and his teaching.

Jesus Heals a Centurion's Servant, 7:1–10

This incident has its source in the Q document. Although the dialogue is the same in both Matthew and Luke, the details differ. A similar story of Jesus' cure of an officer's son is found in John 4:46–53. Common to all three Gospel accounts is the power of Jesus' word. He cures the dying person from a distance. Luke's account is unique in that Jesus does not even meet the Roman officer. The Roman sends two delegations in his stead. The first delegation is made up of some Jewish leaders who intercede on his behalf, pointing out that his affection for the Jewish people is concretely expressed in the help he gave in building the local synagogue (7:4–5).

As Jesus approached the home of the centurion, he was met by a second delegation of friends. They tell Jesus that their friend does not want Jesus to risk ritual uncleanness by entering a Gentile home. More importantly the friends of the officer convey his message of faith: just as he has authority over his men, so he recognizes a greater authority in Jesus to cure sickness by command. Jesus' response praises the faith of the Roman officer by declaring that it has no equivalent, not even in Israel. It is the faith by which a person totally entrusts himself or herself to Jesus. Luke is pointing out to his largely Gentile audience that God finds all people capable of deep faith, Jew or Gentile.

Jesus Raises a Widow's Only Son to Life, 7:11–17

The centurion's servant was "very dear" to him. Now Jesus encounters a funeral procession about to bury the "only son of a woman who was a widow (7:12). This incident is only recorded by Luke. The story conveys the Lucan theme of Jesus' deeply felt compassion for the suffering. Jesus, his "heart filled with pity for her," tenderly requests, "Don't cry" (7:13). As Elijah raised the widow's son from death and took him back to his mother (1 Kgs 17:23), Jesus does the same for the widow of Nain (7:15). Luke further develops the parallel between Elijah and Jesus. Centuries earlier the widow recognized Elijah as a prophet of God (1 Kgs 17:24); now the crowd proclaims that God has again sent a great prophet to his people (7:16). This sign prepares the reader for Jesus' answer to the disciples of John. They can report to John what they have seen—the dead are raised to life (7:22). Typically Luke notes the response of the people: filled with religious awe, they praise God (7:16).

The Messengers Sent by John the Baptist, 7:18–35

Why did the Baptist send disciples to ask Jesus whether or not he was the expected Messiah? This episode reveals some of the uncertainty of the early Church regarding the role of John in relationship to Jesus. Perhaps John's question reflects something of the difference between Jesus' ministry and the rather harsh expectation of the Messiah of judgment whom John had described:

> *The ax is ready to cut down trees at the roots. . . . He has his winnowing shovel with him, to thresh out all the grain and gather the wheat into his barn; but he will burn the chaff in a fire that never goes out (3:9–17).*

Jesus did have hard words for those who were satisfied with the status quo, and he pronounced his woes against the rich, the self-sufficient and the proud (6:24–26), but he was compassionate and merciful toward those whom society dismissed as sinners and outcasts (5:31–32; 7:41–50). Jesus answers John's question by reminding them of his powerful deeds and life-giving preaching, which they themselves have seen and heard. His admonition to the Baptist, "How happy is he who has no doubts about me," may well be an invitation to reconsider his view of Jesus as a prophet of doom or as a "fire and brimstone" Messiah. Not only has Jesus done the messianic deeds of healing described by Isaiah (see Is 26:19; 29:18; 35:5–6; 61:1), but he has done more than Israel had hoped for, because he has also cleansed the lepers and raised the dead to life (5:13; 7:15). This additional beatitude (7:23) provides encouragement also for the members of the churches whom Luke addresses. There will be joy in life for those who do not lose faith in Jesus.

Jesus then turns to the crowds and questions them about their expectations of John the Baptist (7:24–26). All agree that John is a prophet (an exceptional event at that time because for centuries there had been no prophets). Jesus then cites the prophet Malachi and declares that John is the one Malachi had spoken of regarding the messenger God would send to prepare the way for the Messiah (7:27). John is certainly a great man. But even though he is the most extraordinary of mortal men, anyone who belongs to the kingdom is of even greater importance. That is the measure of the significance of the new age introduced by Jesus!

In verses 29–30 Luke reports on the two kinds of responses made to John. The common people and the despised tax gatherers had recognized God speaking through John and repented; the religious leaders had refused to recognize God's authority in John and so they refused to undergo the baptism of repentance. Jesus, however, seems to have been less "successful" than John. The initial enthusiastic response to Jesus (4:14–15) is fading away. Jesus' comparison of the people of his day with the children in the marketplace (7:31–34) is the first indication that Luke gives of widespread non-acceptance of the teaching of Jesus. The people, seeing John fasting in the desert, declared that he was demon-possessed. Seeing Jesus, who shared ordinary food and drink with the socially unacceptable people of his day, the same people ridiculed him for being a wine-drinker and "a friend of tax collectors and outcasts" (7:34). This section closes with an affirmation of God's power. God's wise purpose will be recognized by those willing to accept his plan (7:35).

Simon the Pharisee, the Sinful Woman and Jesus, 7:36–50

OVERVIEW. This story of the righteous Pharisee, the repentant woman and Jesus is another illustration of Luke's ordering the tradition to fit the needs of the believers in the local churches for whom Luke is writing. All four evangelists deal with an incident in which a woman anoints Jesus, and they all treat the incident in a different way. Mark, for example, tells of an unknown woman who anoints the head of Jesus in preparation for his burial; she is not referred to as a sinner (Mk 14:3–9). Luke depicts a sinful woman (perhaps a woman in a socially unacceptable living arrangement, perhaps a prostitute) who seeks out Jesus and then emotionally anoints his feet with ointment. In the oral repetition of this incident (or incidents) it appears that certain facets of the story dropped out and other facets were embellished. Perhaps Luke added the parable that names the Pharisee as Simon (7:40–43).

The way each evangelist positions this story tells us something about their individual concerns. By placing the incident of the repentant woman at the beginning of Jesus' ministry, Luke takes it out of the context of Jesus' death and burial. Thus Luke turns it into a story centering on the attitude of Jesus toward those whom society rejects on the basis of their sinfulness.

COMMENTARY. Jesus was dining at the home of Simon. To the surprise of all an uninvited woman, unnamed and described as living a sinful life (7:37), enters, intending to anoint Jesus' feet. Perhaps she had heard Jesus speak earlier and had been so moved that she wanted to show her gratitude. As she bent over to anoint Jesus' feet (he was probably reclining at table as was the fashion), she began crying, with her tears falling on his feet. Wiping the tears away with her long hair, she kissed Jesus' feet and then completed her anointing. It was a deeply moving gesture on the part of this woman, but Simon's narrow perspective prevents him from seeing the deep implications of the woman's action. Simon focuses on what he sees as Jesus' failure to perceive the woman's sinfulness. Jesus, however, not only understands the kind of woman she is, but also recognizes that she wants to repent. Jesus then tells Simon a parable about two debtors, each of whom owe different amounts and each of whom is forgiven the debt. Since Jesus asks Simon which debtor would love more (7:42), and since Jesus refers to the woman's love (7:47), it seems that this woman had accepted Jesus' teaching about his loving Father, went through a conversion experience, and decided to love God in return.

Simon has a problem: he cannot understand what forgiveness is all about. Simon is a good man. A leader in the community, he is rich in virtue and in the knowledge of the law. But in one way he is worse off than the sinful woman: he does not recognize that he too needs God's forgiveness. If he could recognize his own needy situation, he would be able to accept other people as they receive forgiveness from God. While the sinful woman accepts God in terms of Jesus' teaching—God as loving and forgiving—Simon does not.

The climax to this scene is Jesus' declaration that "the great love she has shown proves that her many sins have been forgiven" (7:47). God has taken the initiative in her life; God forgave her. Her love is her response to God's forgiving initiative. In declaring that her love proves that she has been forgiven, Jesus indicates that her encounter with God's mercy happened before she came to Simon's home! Her sins had already been forgiven by God and her action of anointing Jesus' feet is a demonstration of her earlier repentance. It is obvious to Jesus that her sins had already been taken away—that is why she is able to express her love for God and for God's prophet, Jesus of Nazareth, in the way she has done. Thus Jesus publicly tells her, "Your sins are forgiven" (7:48).

At this point the others present at the banquet object, because they, like Simon their host, are unable to recognize God's work of forgiveness as having taken place in the woman (7:49). At this point Jesus does not argue with those objecting, "Who is this, who even forgives sins?" Instead Jesus reassures the woman, by declaring, "Your faith has saved you; go in peace" (7:50). We may ask, "What was her faith?" We may answer that her faith was her acceptance of Jesus' teaching that God loves every single human person and that God readily forgives those who turn from sin as they turn to him. Having believed that message of

Jesus, she repented and in that repentance found salvation. Knowing that she is totally acceptable to God, she is able "to go in peace" (7:50).

REFLECTION. Reading between the lines, we can see that Luke is concerned about those Christians who tended to look down upon others whose life-styles were less than virtuous. Through this incident Luke makes the point that Jesus is the one through whom God grants salvation to all people—the virtuous and the sinful, the well-to-do and the poor, Jew and Gentile. Perhaps some of the leaders in the various local churches could see themselves mirrored in the indignant righteousness of Simon the Pharisee. What kind of impact could this account have upon us in our day? How many of our own parish communities would be able to extend a warm welcome to a repentant prostitute, a former drug addict, or an ex-convict? Would we be able to accept their very act of coming to our places of worship as the demonstration that God had already forgiven them their sins, and that they are now responding in love? On the other hand, we may consider the sinfulness of those who pass judgment on others. God alone knows the mind and heart. No one else does. Perhaps being judgmental is a sin of no small consequence, for it separates us from God by taking his role and it separates us from our neighbor by lessening their dignity as persons in our own consciousness.

The Woman Who Accompanied Jesus, 8:1–3

COMMENTARY. In these three verses we find that women participated in the evangelizing efforts of Jesus and the twelve as they went about proclaiming the kingdom of God. The women are apparently unrelated to the members of the group, and their presence was therefore at variance with the social patterns of that day. The three women named and the "many other women" provided Jesus with material support (8:3). Luke thus gives us an interesting detail regarding the sources of the financial means that Jesus and his disciples needed to carry on their ministry. Mary of Magdala has no obvious connection with the sinful woman who anointed Jesus' feet at the home of Simon the Pharisee (7:36–50). Mary and Joanna are among the women who are the first to hear the news that Jesus is risen (24:1, 10).

REFLECTION. Regarding the status of women in the Church, it seems that the issue is coming full circle. In the Christian Scriptures, particularly in Luke's account of the Gospel, we find a sense of the equality of all people, Jew or Gentile, slave or free, man or woman. However, the openness toward women demonstrated by Jesus and somewhat practiced in the early Church clashed with the subordination of women to men that was embedded in the cultural mores of the Jewish and Greco-Roman societies. As generations passed, the equality of men and women that was introduced by Jesus in his radical vision of society under God's will (the kingdom of God) gave way as Christians came to accept the prevailing cultural views that saw women as inferior to men. In recent decades, however, the vision of Jesus regarding the relationship of equality between men and women has been rediscovered. As a result, members of the Church, particularly in the Catholic Church in the United States, are raising questions about the full range of rights and responsibilities of the woman as person in the life of the Church.

While the Catholic Church as an institution has manifested some narrow and biased attitudes toward women, there have been instances in which the Church has been in the vanguard of the movement for the recognition of the equality of men and women. In the early 1960s, at the same time the issue of woman's rights entered the arena of public discussion in the United States, Pope John XXIII pointed out that "women are becoming ever more conscious of their human dignity," thereby seeking rights "befitting of a human person both in domestic and public life" (*Pacem in Terris*, #41). At Vatican II the conciliar bishops declared that "every type of discrimination . . . is to be overcome and eradicated as contrary to God's intent" (*Pastoral Constitution on the Church in the Modern World*, #29). In spite of the fact that the 1976 statement of the Sacred Congregation for the Doctrine of the Faith decided that women were not to be ordained as priests, the statement did acknowledge a facet of the Gospel that has deep implications for us all, namely, that Jesus "deliberately and courageously broke" Jewish traditions that discriminated against women. It is noteworthy that the roles of women are being examined in a pastoral letter on women in society and in the Church. Our Church, in its institutional aspects, is being challenged to recognize that sexism is a disservice to the life and message of Jesus. In our day clergy and laity have an opportunity to reexamine long-held attitudes and practices regarding women in order to discern what has been derived from cultural developments and what has its source in the Gospel of Jesus the Christ.

The Parable of the Sower and Its Explanation 8:14–18

OVERVIEW. From 8:4 through 9:50 Luke basically follows Mark's account of Jesus' Galilean ministry (Mk 4:1–9:41). However, Luke omits a large section of Mark's account (Mk

6:45—8:26) and also leaves out two of the three Markan parables, retaining only the parable of the sower and its explanation. To this Luke adds the episode of what can be called "Jesus' true family" (8:19–21), which is found in Mark and Matthew, but in different contexts.

COMMENTARY. The story of the sower is the first parable of Jesus that Luke reports. The parable was a familiar type of Jewish teaching, taking the form of a comparison, a proverb, or a story drawn from everyday life. The parables of Jesus are not all unique; some similar stories are found in the teachings of the rabbis.

During the time of Jesus, farmers sometimes plowed the land after the seeds were scattered. Thus some fell on paths worn through the field, some on thin soil, and so forth. Luke omits Mark's mentioning of the various increases of thirty, sixty, and one hundredfold, mentioning only the hundredfold increase. The point made is that seed sown on good soil yields an abundant crop (8:8).

Following Mark, Luke continues with a statement on the purpose of telling parables (8:9–10) and with an explanation of the parable of the sower (8:11–15). Biblical scholarship distinguishes two different settings: (1) the telling of the parable by Jesus in its original context; (2) the interpretation of the parable as it was understood by the early missionaries and the writers of the Gospel accounts. Recall that Jesus was speaking to "a great crowd" (8:4). Some believe him and follow; others do not. Jesus may have been pointing out that just as the stony nature of the Palestinian soil results in the loss of some of the effort involved in sowing, so the hardness of the heart of many in his Jewish audience causes a lack of response to Jesus' preaching. Those who are open to his message will understand and respond

(8:9); those who are not open to Jesus will find his teaching impossible to understand (8:10).

The second setting deals with the audience for whom the evangelist is writing. We can see much evidence—already present in Mark but more pronounced in Matthew and Luke—of the community's catechetical use of the parables of Jesus. Luke hands these parables on in the context of an expanding mission to the Gentiles and in the context of frequent persecution of the Christian communities. Hence, the parables are retold and interpreted in the 80s to encourage the believing communities whose members were often disappointed in their hopes for the final coming of Jesus and frequently persecuted because they were suspected of being disloyal to the emperor. Luke uses the parables to help explain to his audience the mystery of the kingdom and the magnificence of God's plan.

In the explanation of the parable Luke implies that Jesus is the sower. Only Luke clearly identifies the seed with "the word of God" (8:11). The parable has become an allegory, in which each image represents something else. Thus the seed corresponds to the word of God, and what happens to the seed corresponds to the different ways people respond to God's word. In this explanation (which is possibly the early Church's adaptation of the parable) the recipients are all believers; they are already members of the Church. At stake is the quality of their hearing the word of God. The first group consists of those who hear the word but the devil takes the word "away from their hearts" (8:12). Luke's wording here and in verse 15 catches our attention, reminding us that Mary treasured "all these things in her heart" (2:51). Unless the word of God is treasured within the heart or retained in an obedient heart, it can be snatched away.

The second group falls away in the time of testing.

Threatened by persecution, some believers were driven away from Jesus. Facing the loss of social standing, boycott and imprisonment, some of Jesus' followers gave up their faith.

The third group is described as those who allow their fruit to be choked by worries, riches and pleasures. They hear the word of God and respond to it. Yet they do not protect the tender fruit from the choking power of worldly concerns. The result is that their fruit never ripens (8:14).

The final group persists until they do bear fruit (8:15). These remain steadfast in their faith, exemplifying the Lukan theme of perseverance through every situation. Mary's acceptance of God's will (1:38) may be intended by Luke as a model for those who retain the word of God "in a good and obedient heart" (8:15).

REFLECTION. Some of the details in this passage give us an important perspective on the situation of the early Church. Often we tend to romanticize the lives of the first Christians, envisioning them as living trouble-free lives of love and devotion. The way the parable of the sower was interpreted reveals how the followers of Jesus were pressured from without and tempted from within to let go of their commitment to Jesus and his community. By means of the Church's adaptation of the parable of the sower to a new situation, the risen Lord exhorted his disciples to hear the word and hold it so faithfully that no affliction or persecution could threaten their fidelity.

COMMENTARY. Luke completes the section on the parable of the sower with three verses which illustrate the value of listening intently (8:16–18). In Mark these words are addressed to the crowd, but Luke reports that Jesus speaks directly to the disciples. It would be folly to place a lamp under a bed. A lamp ought to be placed so that it can be useful to people "as they come in" (8:16). The people coming in refers to the Gentiles entering the kingdom. The point of 8:18 is this: attend and appreciate the word of God that has been given lest one's inattentiveness cause the loss of everything.

Jesus' Mother and Brothers, 8:19–21

As we have seen, it is often helpful to compare how Luke has used a particular remembrance with one of the other evangelists. These comparisons enable us to grasp the reasons why Luke used and adapted a word or deed of Jesus for the sake of his readers. Reading Mark 3:21–22, 31–35, one finds that the relatives of Jesus, among whom are his mother and brothers (or cousins), seek to "take charge of him, convinced he was out of his mind" (Mk 3:21). When they arrive at the place where Jesus is teaching, he is informed of their presence. Jesus seems to disassociate himself from his family by indicating that those gathered about him are his mother and brothers because they are hearing the word of God (Mk 3:31–35). Then Mark goes on to take up the parable about the sower and the seed, but in a setting different from that in which Jesus' mother and brothers appeared (Mk 4:14ff).

Luke takes his basic information from Mark but rearranges the details and the sequence. Luke places Mary's arrival after the parable of the sower and its explanation (8:4–15). Mary is thus associated with the different ways people respond to the words of God, for Jesus says, "My mother and brothers are those who hear the word of God and obey it" (8:21). Once again Luke presents the mother of Jesus as a model of the disciple who lives a life of obedience to the word of God (see 1:38; 2:19, 51).

Jesus Calms a Storm, 8:22–25

In this episode Luke abbreviates Mark, dropping out many details. For example, the disciples' gruff remark, "Teacher, don't you care that we are about to die?" (Mk 4:38) becomes, "Master, Master! We are about to die" (8:24). Jesus' rebuke "Where is your faith?" (8:25) is gentler than Mark's observation that the disciples had not even begun to believe (Mk 4:40).

The amazed response and questioning among the disciples, "Who is this man?" (8:25), implies that they are beginning to see that Jesus is human but somehow more than human. Step by step they come to realize the uniqueness of Jesus. The power of God as Lord of the storm is seen as present in Jesus (see Is 51:9f; Pss 89:8, 93:3f). The basic meaning of this episode is not to prove that Jesus is God (faith cannot be elicited by sheer acts of power) but to indicate that the power of God is with Jesus.

Jesus Heals a Demon-Possessed Man, 8:26–39

This episode has many difficulties for the interpreter. Like the stilling of the storm, this is an account of the power of God acting through Jesus. The difficulty in comprehending the text is reflected in Luke's own uncertainty regarding the number of demons possessing the man living in the burial caves in the territory of the Geresenes. Is it one demon, as indicated throughout verse 29, or are there many demons, as depicted in 8:27, 30 and following?

The description of the demon's activity prior to the arrival of Jesus (8:29) indicates that the man suffered from possession or from a severe mental disorder. In a culture in which the evils of human sickness and disorder were not distinguished from demonic possession, Jesus was recognized as both healer and exorcist. He was perceived as a person victorious over any forces that debased a person's human dignity.

The demons' request that they not be sent to the abyss (8:31) is a reflection of the first century world-picture that imaged the underworld as the place for the confinement of evil spirits. Jesus' permitting the demons to move from the man to the herd of pigs can be variously interpreted. There could be a connection between the man's ritual uncleanness (he lives in the burial caves) and the swine which were regarded as unclean animals. The Jews regarded pigs as likely habitations for demons. Perhaps the transfer of the evil spirits from the possessed man to the herd of pigs was proof that the man was cured by Jesus. The incident may have been connected with an underlying popular belief that demons could be destroyed in water.

More to the point is what happened to the man who had been possessed. The townspeople came and found the man "sitting at the feet of Jesus, clothed, and in his right mind" (8:35). Luke adds the detail of the man sitting at Jesus' feet, the position of the disciple. An astonishing transformation has taken place, and the people respond in fear and awe as they recognize the presence of God's power (8:35).

The account ends in both acceptance and rejection. The people ask Jesus to leave, but the man who had been exorcised wants to "go with" Jesus, a request indicative of his willingness to be a disciple. Jesus does depart, but not before he leaves the cured man behind as a witness to the merciful power of God (8:39).

Jesus Heals Jairus' Daughter and the Woman Who Touched His Cloak, 8:40–56

In these two cures Luke follows Mark with little change. Mark sometimes places a story within a story. In this case, Jairus, a ruler of the local synagogue, desperately pleads with Jesus to heal his dying daughter. Luke adds the detail that she is his "only daughter" (8:42). As Jesus makes his way to the home of Jairus, a second incident is narrated, the story of a woman who was cured by touching Jesus' cloak (8:44–48).

The response of Jesus in 8:45–46 has long interested commentators and scholars. Jesus stated that he felt power go out of him and yet he did not know who touched him. This is a very early view of Jesus; he is depicted as one who does not have complete control over his ability to heal. As Mark and Luke portray it, Jesus' healing power was something people could take from him. It indicates a dimension of mystery in Jesus' own life. The woman, perhaps suffering from a uterine hemorrhage, was ritually unclean. She would have been excluded from worshiping at the temple for the last twelve years of her life. It is no wonder that when she admits her deed, she is trembling at Jesus' feet. When she publicly—"in front of everybody"—tells of her intention and subsequent cure, Jesus declares that it was her faith that made her well. She had believed that God acted through Jesus and thus she experienced a double transformation, from sickness to health and from fear to peace (8:47–48).

Verse 49 returns to the narrative regarding Jairus' daughter. She is now dead. There is a finality in the message that tells Jairus there is no more hope. But Jesus invites him to believe that she will be well. In light of 8:48

Jairus is being asked to have faith in God acting through Jesus. When Jesus says that the girl is not dead but sleeping, he is declaring that God has power over death and can wake a person from death itself. Those standing about lack this faith and therefore ridicule Jesus. They have seen her die and know she is dead, not sleeping. Jesus touches the child's hand and her life returns. Although Luke usually concludes such healing episodes by mentioning the praising of God by the witnesses, here he finishes as Mark did, with Jesus asking for silence (8:56; Mk 5:43). This request for silence, frequently found in Mark and occasionally included by Luke, is called by many scholars "the messianic secret." By way of explanation it appears that Jesus was reluctant to encourage his people's messianic expectations. Thus he sometimes tried to keep his messianic mission secret. The people wanted an anointed one who would be triumphant, a nationalistic liberator who would deliver Israel from the harsh Roman occupation. Jesus resisted the tempter in the desert, and during the course of his ministry he resists the desires of his people who want a Messiah on their own terms.

Week Four

During this week we shall see that Jesus' Galilean ministry is drawing to a close (9:1–50). Luke concludes Jesus' preaching in Galilee by recounting five climactic incidents, each of which looks forward to his passion and resurrection narrative. The sending forth of the twelve in 9:1–6 is related to the commissioning of Jesus' followers as witnesses in 24:45–49. The sharing of food in 9:10–17 correlates with the Last Supper in 22:14–23. Peter's profession of faith in Jesus as Messiah in 9:18–21 parallels the testing of Peter's faith in 22:31–34, 54–62. Jesus' announcements of his passion in 9:22, 43–45 correspond with his suffering and death in 22:63—23:46. Finally, the transfiguration in 9:28–36 is a prelude to Jesus' resurrection and ascension in 24:1–51.

Having instructed seventy-two disciples, Jesus sends them in pairs to proclaim the good news of the approaching kingdom of God (10:1–16). As opposition to Jesus increases, a lawyer attempts to discredit him. This leads to the telling of the powerful story of the neighborly Samaritan (10:25–37). At the home of Martha Jesus reveals that one loves God by attending to his teachings (10:38–42). This fourth week of study closes with Jesus giving his disciples the prayer that uniquely expresses their identity: the Lord's Prayer (11:2–4).

DAILY STUDY ASSIGNMENTS: WEEK FOUR

Day	Luke	Commentary
1	9:1–27	pp. 98–105
2	9:28–50	pp. 105–109
3	9:51—10:24	pp. 110–116
4	10:25–37	pp. 116–120
5	10:38—11:12	pp. 120–128

6 Review Luke 9:1—11:12 in light of the reflection questions.

7 Group meets for study and sharing.

1. What are some of the ways we can carry on the mission of healing that was first given to the twelve (9:6)?

2. As contemporary disciples of Jesus, what are some of the ways we can take up the cross "every day"?

3. Reflect on the transfiguration of Jesus. How does this scene give you a sense of hope and the courage to continue following him as his disciple?

4. Early Christianity was referred to as "the Way." In light of Luke's telling much of the story of Jesus in terms of his journey to Jerusalem, can you think of yourself as a wayfarer too? Why or why not?

5. What is the point of the three discipleship stories in 9:57–62? In what way or ways do these stories speak to you in your particular circumstances of life?

6. "Good Samaritan" is a term commonly used to describe the person who takes the time to help others. Based on the lawyer's question "Who is my neighbor?" what other meanings is this parable intended to have?

Jesus Sends Out the Twelve, 9:1–6

COMMENTARY. We have seen that Jesus gathered disciples (5:1–6, 11), chose twelve of them as symbols for the foundation of the new Israel (6:12–16), and began to form apostles and disciples into a community. These Galilean men and women would serve as witnesses to what he did and said (see 8:1–21). Now, in this last section dealing with the Galilean ministry (9:1–50), Jesus sends the twelve as missionaries. As he does so, he commissions the twelve to do what he did—to exorcise demons, cure the sick and proclaim the kingdom of God. At the very outset of his ministry Jesus stated that he had come to fulfill the promise made by God through the prophet Isaiah: "He has sent me to bring the good news to the poor, to proclaim liberty to captives and to the blind new sight and to set the downtrodden free, to proclaim the Lord's year of favor" (Is 61:1–2; Lk 4:17–18). Now Jesus gives the disciples "the power and authority" to participate in his mission (9:1). Note the connection between healing and preaching the kingdom of God (9:2). By relating these two activities Jesus indicates that the kingdom is not only a spiritual and inward endeavor but also one that takes into consideration the total person, the renewal of the person in both body and soul. To proclaim God's kingdom is to announce that God's saving initiative is about to take place. God's reign of justice, a reign characterized by right relationships between God and his people, and between each person and his or her neighbor, is about to begin.

Jesus instructs his disciples to take nothing with them (9:3). This indicates the urgency of the moment. They shall rely completely on God who will supply them with their needs through those willing to welcome them and the message they preach (9:3–4).

The six verses of 9:1–6 convey much of the tenor of the ministry of Jesus in the years 28–30 A.D. We can envision Jesus as a traveling preacher, moving from one place to another, proclaiming the Father's will to all who would listen. Jesus preached in the prophetic style, challenging people to reform their lives in view of the compassionate love of God and the coming of his reign, his kingdom. If people do not welcome and listen to the disciples, they must move on down the road, shaking the dust from their feet as the pious Jew would shake the dust of the Gentile countryside from his feet upon returning to the soil of Israel (9:5). Luke then hints at a universal aspect to the disciples' mission by noting that they preached and healed "everywhere" (9:6).

REFLECTION. Because we are the Church, the mission of Jesus is our mission as well. We can ask ourselves if we have taken seriously our capacities for healing one another. Do we rely on both prayer and medicine? The gathered family praying for the sick member and the husband or wife praying with each other for the restoration of health can be both an expression of faith and a participation in the healing ministry that belongs to us as Church. For those of us who have eyes to see, opportunities for continuing the healing ministry of Jesus are many. We will find them in caring for a child's skinned knee, in the praying for the healing of hurtful memories, and in the parish's ministry to the sick.

The Confusion of Herod, 9:7–9

COMMENTARY. Upon hearing about all the things that were happening (a reference to the preaching and healing deeds of Jesus) Herod Antipas tries to understand. Some people are saying that Jesus is Elijah, one of the prophets or John the Baptist come back to life. Herod dismisses these explanations, noting the finality with which he had ended John's ministry. Thus Herod was left with the abiding question: "But who is this man I hear these things about?" These three verses prepare us for the question Jesus will soon ask of his disciples in 9:18–20. Herod will later achieve his goal of seeing Jesus (9:9 and 23:8–12), but it will avail him nothing because he refuses to accept Jesus' signs as manifestations of God's kingdom breaking into history.

Jesus Feeds the Five Thousand, 9:10–17

Having completed their mission, the twelve return, recounting to Jesus what they had done. The feeding of the five thousand is the only miracle story common to all four accounts of the Gospel. It is the culmination of Jesus' Galilean ministry, since after this Jesus concentrates upon instructing the twelve.

Note the similarity between the account of Jesus' feeding of this great crowd and an event described in 2 Kings. It seems that when the early preachers proclaimed the good news of Jesus to the Jews, they modeled the great sharing of food upon a format that their audience could easily recognize. Thus the event is described in a way that helps the listeners understand its meaning. Notice how this theme of God's providing for the needs of his people is demonstrated in the recounting of how both Elisha and Jesus saw to it that the hungry were fed:

Another time, a man came .... bringing Elisha twenty loaves of bread made from the first barley harvested that year, and some . . . grain. Elisha told his servant to feed the group of prophets with this, but he answered, "Do you think this is enough for a hundred men?"

Elisha replied, "Give it to them to eat, because the Lord says that they will eat and still have some left over." So the servant set the food before them, and as the Lord had said, they all ate, and there was still some left over (2 Kgs 4:42–44).

But Jesus said to them, "You yourselves give them something to eat."

They answered, "All we have are five loaves and two fish. Do you want us to go and buy food for this whole crowd?"

Jesus said to his disciples, "Make the people sit down. . . ." . . . Jesus took the five loaves . . . thanked God for them, broke them, and gave them to the disciples to distribute to the people.

They all ate and had enough, and the disciples took up twelve baskets of what was left over (9:13–17).

This text not only recalls the past history of Israel but also makes a statement about discipleship and looks to the future event in which Jesus will give himself at the Last Supper. The reply of the disciples in 9:13 indicates that without Jesus, what they have is insufficient. After Jesus asks the disciples for what food they have, he blesses it, gives it back to them and they distribute enough for all. These actions model the proper relationship between Jesus and his followers. If they rely upon Jesus and his power, they will have what they need to minister to others. It is such dependence upon God that is the foundation of the disciples' effective service.

The Greek word for thanksgiving is *eucharistia*. Luke anticipates Jesus' gift of the bread of the Eucharist by using the same sequence of words on three separate occasions. In the feeding of the five thousand, in the institution of the Eucharist at the Last Supper and at the breaking of the bread in the Emmaus supper, the same words occur in the same sequence:

> *Jesus took the five loaves . . . thanked God for them, broke them and gave . . . (9:16).*

> *Then he took a piece of bread, gave thanks to God, broke it, and gave it to them . . . (22:19).*

> *He sat down to eat with them, took the bread, and said the blessing; then he broke the bread and gave it to them (24:30).*

Peter's Declaration of Faith, 9:18–20

After Luke recounts the feeding of the great crowd, he skips over a large section of material in Mark's account (Mk 6:45—8:26). It was Mark's plan to show how the rejection of Jesus by his people in Galilee led him to further journeying, including travels in non-Jewish territory. Luke omits this section of Mark, probably in favor of showing that Jesus now turned to intense instruction of his disciples.

The crux of this episode is found in the two questions Jesus asks of his disciples. Luke, in order to indicate how important these questions are, points out that Jesus was praying immediately before he asked them (9:18). First Jesus asked his followers about the opinion of the crowds regarding his identity. The answer they give is an echo of Herod's puzzlement (9:79). Perhaps many people were impressed by Jesus' signs and esteemed him as a prophet (9:19). However, they did not make the further commitment of putting faith in Jesus. The second question asks the disciples for their perception of Jesus' identity: "Who do you say I am?" In a very real way Luke's entire narrative deals with the answer to this question, for the answer can be found only in an account "of the things that have taken place among us" (1:1). Peter speaks for the twelve, declaring his faith: "You are God's Messiah."

Jesus Speaks of Himself as the Suffering Messiah, 9:21-27

Jesus is indeed "God's Messiah," but in a way that none expect. For this reason he warns his disciples not to speak of him as the Messiah (9:21). God's Anointed One must follow a path of suffering, for only in this manner would the Scriptures be fulfilled (9:22). This is the first time that Jesus speaks of his passion and death. Luke relates it closely with the event of the transfiguration soon to follow (9:28-36).

Having spoken to his disciples about the Son of Man's being called to be the suffering Messiah, Jesus turns to the crowd and speaks to them about the meaning of discipleship (9:23). While basically following Mark, Luke makes several changes that indicate his own perspective on discipleship. Note that Luke adds the phrase "every day" to the saying of Jesus reported in Mark 8:34. Thus Luke teaches that the cross-bearing of the disciples is not limited to a single significant moment but must become an on-going, day to day way of following Jesus (9:23). The phrase "every day" indicates Luke's perspective on the Church: the community of disciples must live in history rather than awaiting an immediate return of its Lord in glory.

The saying of Jesus in verse 24 is found in all four accounts of the Gospel. It expresses a fundamental attitude of Jesus that reverses the seemingly common sense values held by most people: if one wants to save one's life, one must be willing to lose it (9:24). While Mark has Jesus speaking about the one willing to lose his life "for me and for the gospel" (Mk 8:35), Luke omits "and for the gospel," thereby stressing single-minded commitment to the person of Jesus. The rhetorical question of 9:25 points out the importance of making a commitment to Jesus—it would be stupidity to gain the world while losing one's self. Verse 26 heightens even further the crucial importance of choosing Jesus and living out his teachings.

The statement regarding the presence of some of Jesus' hearers who will not die until they have seen the kingdom of God is subject to various interpretations. Perhaps it represents an isolated saying of Jesus which Mark added to his account in spite of the fact that it did not connect clearly to its context. Some see verse 27 as a reference to Peter, James and John who see in the transfiguration of Jesus a vision of his end-time glory (9:28–29).

REFLECTION. While Dr. Martin Luther King, Jr. was not a perfect disciple of Jesus, he tried to follow his Master. Martin had committed his sins, but hoped that God would judge him on "the total bent" of his life. Three years before he was murdered, King spoke his mind in a way that carried a contemporary expression of what Jesus long ago said about the person who was willing to lose his life (9:24). Martin declared:

The only way we can really achieve freedom is to somehow conquer the fear of death. For if a man has not discovered something that he will die for, he isn't fit to live. Deep down in our non-violent creed is the conviction there are some things so dear, some things so precious, some things so utterly true, that they are worthwhile dying for.

The Transfiguration, 9:28–36

COMMENTARY. In all three Synoptic accounts the transfiguration is placed in this same position: immediately following Peter's profession of faith in Jesus as the Messiah, the first teaching about his death and coming in glory. Following these pivotal events Jesus takes Peter, James and John to a mountaintop in order to pray (9:28).

In this manifestation of the divinity (glory) of Jesus, one finds a blending of biblical symbolism, theological statement and religious experience. It will not do to simply read and reenact this scene in the eye of one's mind. The episode must be explored in the context of both Judaism and the Gospel. Mountains are often symbols of unique encounters with God. Moses received the law on Mount Sinai (Ex 19:1—20:21). Elijah had an encounter with God on the top of a mountain (1 Kgs 19:11–13). On this mountain, the three disciples are privileged to witness the changes that take place in Jesus' face and his clothes (9:29). The change in his countenance and clothing anticipates Jesus' coming in glory (9:26) and also looks ahead to the transformation of Jesus after his resurrection, a change which makes it difficult for the disciples and others to recognize him (24:16).

Moses and Elijah, symbolic figures representing the law and the prophets, speak with Jesus about his death in Jerusalem, which will fulfill God's purpose. Luke alone tells us of the subject matter of the conversation between

Jesus and the two heroes of Israelite history. They literally speak of Jesus' "exodus," his passing over to God through death. Luke wants his readers to understand that Jesus' crucifixion in Jerusalem will be his exodus, his going forth for the salvation of the world. The sleeping apostles awaken just in time to see the transfigured Jesus and the two others. According to some scholars, Luke's reference to the nodding apostles partially explains the fact that they did not understand the necessity of the passion-exodus of Jesus until after he had risen from the dead. Not having heard Moses and Elijah speak with Jesus about his passion and death, Peter misunderstands the meaning of the revelation. It is a moment of glory that Peter wants to prolong by setting up three tents, a practice that was traditional during the Jewish feast of Tabernacles. Luke notes that Peter did not understand what he had proposed (9:33).

The cloud that covered the figures on the mountain symbolizes God's presence (Ex 24:15–18; 40:34). The scene also recalls the manifestation of God at Sinai in which God spoke with Moses in the midst of thunder, fire and smoke enveloping the mountain peak (Ex 19:16–25). The Father's declaration of Jesus' sonship connects this event with Jesus' baptism and the vision Jesus received as he prayed (3:22). The command to listen to Jesus alerts the disciples to remember what Jesus has already taught them and also commands them to pay close attention to what Jesus will say on the journey to Jerusalem which will soon be undertaken (9:51).

Jesus Heals a Possessed Boy 9:37–43; the Second Reference to Jesus' Passion and Death, 9:43–45

As Jesus came down from the mountain, the distraught father of an only son pleads for the cure of his son possessed by an evil spirit (the description of the boy's behavior indicates epilepsy). Jesus had given his disciples power to heal and exorcise (9:1–2), but in this case they were unable. Luke greatly abbreviates Mark's account, and in so doing focuses the reader's attention on the healing power of Jesus. It is not clear whom Jesus addresses in his rebuke, "How unbelieving and wrong you people are!" It could be a complaint against the people who have not responded to Jesus' message, or it could be directed at the disciples. The authority of Jesus that was manifested to the three disciples on the mountain is here manifested to a larger number of people who marvel at the "mighty power of God" (9:43).

In spite of the fact that the people are marveling at "everything" (a reference to the whole public ministry of Jesus) Jesus was doing, Jesus realizes there is another dimension that is unrecognized by his disciples. He is warning his disciples to look beyond the acclaim he receives for his healing deeds. The wording of Jesus' teaching about his betrayal (9:44) is so different from Mark's account that there is reason to think that Luke had access to another tradition, one perhaps closer to the specific teaching of Jesus himself. Note that there are no details about the passion, death or resurrection in Jesus' warning to the disciples— only a vague prediction of his being betrayed and handed over to human power.

Luke underscores the lack of understanding on the part of Jesus' followers (9:45). In view of the very explicit teaching about Jesus' passion in 9:22, there are several possible explanations of the disciples' inability to understand. Perhaps they do not want to understand because of the fearful implications. Perhaps the details of the passion in 9:22 came from the knowledge gained after the fact of Jesus' death and resurrection; this understanding may have then been projected back into the days of Jesus' public ministry by the believing community.

Who Is the Greatest?, 9:46–48; On Using Jesus' Name, 9:49–50

When the disciples argue about their status immediately after Jesus spoke of his betrayal, it is obvious that they did not understand Jesus' identity as servant and suffering Messiah. Their concern for prestige is intuited by Jesus (9:47) who then places a child by his side. In Near Eastern culture a child was held in little regard. By placing a child by his side, Jesus honors the child.

Because a child is a person without means, anyone who helps a child does so not for the sake of reward, but for the sake of the child. Since Jesus identifies himself with the child (whoever welcomes a child in Jesus' name welcomes Jesus), the one who welcomes that child welcomes both Jesus and the Father who sent Jesus (9:48a). The crux of the matter is summed up in the reversal of values in verse 48b: the one who is great is the least among us. Therefore, the disciples are being asked to abandon the concern for prestige and embrace the service of the nobodies of this world, for these are the great ones in the eyes of God and of the one sent by God (9:48).

Verses 49 and 50 have a variety of interpretations. Some see an allusion to early Church controversies regarding those who performed exorcisms in the name of Jesus but without a strong connection with the believing community. On the most obvious level of meaning the apostle John, conscious of the authorization that Jesus gave the twelve (9:1–2), would have the unnamed exorcist cease his activity. Jesus replies that the exorcist should be left alone because he is an ally, not an opponent. According to Mark the words of Jesus read: "Whoever is not against us is for us" (Mk 9:40). Luke changed the wording to read: "Whoever is not against you is for you," thereby making the teaching of Jesus' ministry more applicable to the disciples of Luke's Church in the 80s.

The Journey to Jerusalem, 9:51—19:27

OVERVIEW. Jesus has become aware that he must suffer at the hands of the Jewish leaders. His resolute decision to travel to Jerusalem (9:51) turns the holy city into a symbol of his commitment to fulfill the Father's purpose. In 19:28 Jesus will prepare to enter the city which is both his destination and destiny.

The material found in 9:51 through 18:41 is often called Luke's "special section." The reason for this designation is the fact that Luke has basically used Mark as his source through 9:50, but in 9:51 Luke inserted a large block of his own material. In 18:15 Luke returns to his Markan source. Nearly sixty percent of the material found in this special section is unique to Luke (the rest is drawn from a source which Matthew also used).

From the point Jesus makes up his mind to go to Jerusalem, through his arrival at the place where he will sacrifice himself for the sake of saving the human family, to the moment Jesus ascends to heaven (24:51), Luke depicts

Jesus as a pilgrim, a wayfarer. While he is on the way, particularly in the nine chapters between 9:51 and 18:14, Jesus sets forth the attitudes and values his followers need in journeying through life. Having begun his journey to Jerusalem, Jesus never goes back, never retraces his steps, never even looks behind. Luke presents Jesus as the one model for all disciples. In Luke's account the journey to Jerusalem—culminating in the passion, death, resurrection and ascension—becomes a metaphor for the Christian's journey through life.

A Samaritan Village Refuses Hospitality, 9:51–56

COMMENTARY. The opening verse of this section builds on the conversation between Moses, Elijah and Jesus in the transfiguration scene. Moses and Elijah had spoken of Jesus' passover (9:31). Luke begins by referring to the nearness of Jesus' departure from this world to the Father. The text of the *Today's English Version* translation reads "he made up his mind" (9:51). However, the decision of Jesus has a far more decisive quality than that communicated by the phrase "made up his mind." Jesus' decision parallels a passage in Isaiah 50:7, which the New American Bible translates in this way:

> *I have set my face like flint, knowing that I shall not be put to shame.*

The prophet has decided to stake his whole life on God, trusting that God will vindicate him in the end. Jesus is depicted as doing the same. After the plots, the persecution, and the cross, Jesus too will be vindicated, for God will raise him from the dead. Jesus sets out for Jerusalem, knowing that his life is at stake yet trusting that God will be with him.

The Samaritans, at enmity with the Jews, refuse to welcome Jesus and his followers. Referring to the kind of retribution Elijah called down upon the soldiers of the king of Samaria (2 Kgs 1:9–14), James and John are prepared to ask God to destroy the village (9:54). Jesus rebukes them (9:55). They have obviously failed to understand his teaching on non-retaliation (see 6:27, 6:35 and especially 6:36).

Three Discipleship Stories, 9:57–62

COMMENTARY. The three crisp, rapid incidents in 9:57–62 stress that following Jesus is a life-changing endeavor which demands total commitment. Three men present themselves as candidates for discipleship. In relation to Jesus' recent decision to take a dangerous journey to Jerusalem, it seems that these three men do not realize the intensity of sacrifice involved. Jesus indicates to each one that to follow the Son of Man requires total commitment.

Luke begins this section by noting that Jesus and his disciples were "on their way" (9:57). One of the titles used by the Lucan communities in the decades immediately after Jesus' ascension was "the Way." (See 24:22 in Acts, Luke's sequel to the Gospel.) Luke seems to anticipate the faith journey of the early Church by his wording in 9:57. The man who approaches Jesus wants to be more than a member of the larger group of Jesus' disciples. His request indicates a desire to be a member of the disciples who accompanied Jesus wherever he traveled. Jesus does not belittle the men's enthusiasm, but explains how demanding is the disciple's life—an itinerant existence that compared unfavorably with animals, who had at least their own den or nest.

In the second episode, Jesus himself invites someone to follow (9:59). This man is willing to be a disciple but first wishes to complete his filial duty to his father. Judaism attached great importance to the religious obligation of burying the dead, but Jesus declares that preaching the kingdom takes priority even over that most sacred duty (9:60). The declaration that the dead should bury their own probably refers to those who do not "come alive" by responding to Jesus' invitation to the kingdom of God.

The third incident is unique to Luke. It parallels the incident in which Elijah permitted Elisha to say farewell to his mother and father before he became Elijah's disciple (1 Kgs 19:20). Jesus' call to discipleship is so radical that once one is called there can be no turning back, not even to say farewell to one's family.

REFLECTION. The call to the kingdom is closely related to the call to discipleship. Jesus urgently called people to make a radical decision to accept God's reign over their lives. He declared that the time for deciding is *now*. He challenged his hearers to make a decision to live in a new way beginning in the present moment. He did not call people to decide today because the world would end on the morrow. Rather he called for a decision in the present moment because the acceptance or rejection of his call to follow was seen as the acceptance or rejection of the reign of God in their lives. The basic message of these three stories on discipleship is that nothing else can have the first place in our lives because the first place is already claimed by God's Messiah. If we are complacent about the way we express our commitment to Jesus, the urgency in verses 57–62 might call into question the pattern of our day to day living.

Jesus Sends Out the Seventy-Two, 10:1–16

OVERVIEW. Only Luke recounts this incident—the sending on mission of seventy-two disciples. The instructions of Jesus to the twelve in Matthew's account (Mt 9:37–38 and 10:7–16) are spoken to the seventy-two in Luke's version. Scholars point out that Luke seems to have followed his Markan source for the mission of the twelve (9:1–6 and Mk 6:7–13), and may have based his account of the mission of the seventy-two on material found in the Q document. The advice of Jesus in 10:1–12 may have been given on various occasions and then gathered together in the light of their common theme, namely, instructions for those going on missionary journeys.

The first verse attests to the ancient practice of having two witnesses give testimony in matters of importance. Not only is traveling in pairs an asset in witnessing, it is also a recognition of the need for mutual support. Some see in the number seventy-two a reference to the seventy-two nations in the tenth chapter of Genesis in the Septuagint (Greek) Bible.

The large harvest represents the people living in towns and villages who will hear the message of Jesus regarding the nearness of the kingdom of God. By speaking of God as the owner of the harvest, Jesus indicates that he has come to serve his Father by gathering in the people who belong to his kingdom. Those sent are to pray for additional disciple-missionaries to join them (10:2).

The shift from the imagery of the harvest to that of lambs among wolves suggests opposition and persecution (10:2). As Jesus encountered rejection, so will his disciples (see 6:22–23). The disciples are to travel light, since they must trust in God to provide for their needs. Because of the urgent necessity of their missionary activity, they must not delay by greeting other travelers (10:4).

Verses 5 through 7 tell the disciples how they are to proceed once they reach a town or village. The greeting of peace and the quest for "a peace-loving man" suggest that the missionaries are looking for those open to receiving the good news of God's salvation. The blessing, "Peace be with this house," is more than a wish or hope. In Jewish understanding, the prophetic word carries within itself the power to achieve what it states. Thus, if the person is not a man ready to welcome the good news of salvation, the disciple-missionary is to recall the greeting. The prophetic speaker has power over the word that is spoken.

In 10:8–9 we hear Jesus' instructions regarding what the disciples are to do when they find a town that welcomes them. Note that the disciples are told to heal the sick prior to proclaiming the good news of the kingdom (10:9). The deeds of healing thus function as signs of the presence of God's kingdom.

If the pairs of missionaries are not welcomed, they are to declare to the inhabitants that their refusal prevented their experience of the kingdom. While the message of Jesus can bring peace to house and town (10:6, 8), that peace can exist only on one condition: free acceptance by both the individual and society of the nearness of the kingdom in Jesus (10:11).

In verse 12 the pagan town of Sodom is contrasted with the Jewish towns that will refuse to accept the missionaries sent by Jesus. In 10:13–15 Jesus refers to three towns on the Sea of Galilee which had been the scene of his preaching and marvelous signs. The response of the inhabitants is contrasted unfavorably with the pagan cities of Tyre and Sidon. These two cities would have repented had they had the opportunity to hear Jesus and see his deeds.

Chorazin, Bethsaida and Capernaum, by their refusal to heed Jesus' call to receive the news of the kingdom, have brought judgment upon themselves.

The missionary discourse closes with Jesus' authorization of the seventy-two disciples to preach in his name (10:16).

The Return of the Seventy-Two Disciples, 10:17–20

Luke alone records this scene. The disciples return from their mission, rejoicing about their success in exorcising evil spirits in Jesus' name. Jesus' reference to Satan falling from heaven is difficult to interpret. Jesus may be referring to Isaiah 14:12, which speaks of the death of the king of Babylon in terms of the swift fall of a Phoenician deity (Baal, "the Most High," a would-be rival of Yahweh). The "bright morning star . . . fallen from heaven" (Is 14:12) was identified with Lucifer by some of the Fathers of the Church. The idea of the defeat of one who stood in opposition to God may have been used by Jesus to symbolize the impact of the disciples' exorcisms. The healings are signs of the inbreaking of God's kingdom and the resulting defeat of Satan and his allies. As much as this is a cause for rejoicing, Jesus declares that the greater cause for joy is the inclusion of the disciples in the heavenly book of life. Despite the joy in God's evident power to touch others through their mission, the disciples are to rejoice first in God's mercy in their own lives.

Jesus Thanks His Father, 10:21–24

The prayer of Jesus (10:21) and the subsequent teaching are taken from the Q source, which Luke and Matthew both utilize. Luke characteristically adds the detail that Jesus "was filled with joy by the Holy Spirit" (10:21). The prayer of Jesus, expressing his gratitude that the Father chooses to reveal himself to the unlearned, is very typical of Luke's portrait of Jesus. Luke has pointed out the role of the Spirit in Jesus' life (1:35, 41; 2:25–27; 4:1, 14, 18). Now he underscores Jesus' relationship with his Father. Verse 22 states that the authority of Jesus is based on his intimate relationship with his heavenly Father. Thus he can reveal the Father to those he calls.

Soon Jesus will be teaching his disciples to pray, "Father: May your holy name be honored" (11:2). At the end of his life Jesus will pray, "Father! In your hands I place my spirit!" (23:46). Humility and trustful dependence upon the Father are crucial virtues for those to whom "the knowledge of the secrets of the kingdom of God" (8:9–10) is given. The self-reliant attitude of the wise and learned prevents them from receiving the fullness of God's self-revelation.

In verse 23 Jesus privately declares to his disciples that they are truly blessed because they behold what many in the past have longed to see: God's kingdom breaking into history through the words and deeds of Jesus. God's kingdom has come as pure gift, free, with no strings attached. Such is the Father's amazing grace.

The Parable of the Neighborly Samaritan, 10:25–37

OVERVIEW. The parable of the "Good Samaritan" is the first presentation of three interrelated themes treated in 10:25—11:13. The parable of the Jew who was saved by the Samaritan is told by Jesus in response to the lawyer's question, "Who is my neighbor?" This deals with the relationship of disciple and community. The second theme, dramatized by the account of Jesus' visit to the home of Martha and Mary (10:38–42), deals with an implied question: "What is the relationship between Jesus and his disciples?" The third theme is expressed in Jesus' teaching on prayer (11:1–13) and can be described as answering the question, "What is the proper relationship between the disciples and God, their heavenly Father?"

COMMENTARY. When a teacher of the law comes to ask Jesus about what one must do to inherit eternal life, his intention is to "trap" Jesus. This trapping could refer to an attempt to lessen Jesus' reputation as a teacher by showing that he was not skilled in interpreting the Scriptures. The question that "tests" Jesus is the most significant a person can ask: "What must I do to receive eternal life?" The question recognizes that such life is indeed a gift from God—it can only be received. At the same time, however, there is the crucial element of preparing oneself to receive that gift: "What must I do?"

Jesus replies with his own question, asking the lawyer what he himself reads in the holy Scriptures. Now the lawyer is being tested on his understanding of the law. The lawyer, who recites the great Jewish prayer, the Shema, at least three times a day, cites the portion about loving God with one's whole being (Dt 6:4). He also includes the words of Leviticus 19:18, which ask that one love one's neighbor as oneself.

Jesus has led his questioner to answer his own question regarding the way one must live to prepare for receiving the gift of life eternal: love God with your whole self and love your neighbor as yourself. "Do this," says Jesus, "and you will live" (10:28). The stage is now set for two further questions. The question of "How do I love my neighbor?" will be answered in the parable of the Good Samaritan (10:29–37). The question "How do I love God—in light of the coming of Jesus?" will be answered in the episode of Jesus' visit to the home of Martha and Mary (10:38–42).

Having set out to test Jesus and realizing that he had been tested on his own knowledge of the law, the lawyer tries to save face by asking Jesus, "Who is my neighbor?" Here the lawyer is not seeking a definition as much as he is asking Jesus to set the boundaries between who qualifies as a neighbor and who does not. For many Jewish teachers one's neighbor was limited to those who belonged to the covenant community. Some Jewish authorities restricted the term even further to those of one's own like-minded group, thus enabling the righteous to exclude those Jews who did not practice the law in its fullness. In this way, the Gentiles, the sinners, and the nobodies had no claim on the compassionate love of their supposed "betters." By asking "Who is my neighbor?" the lawyer asks Jesus for his interpretation of where to draw the line.

Jesus will once more lead his questioner to answer his own question. But first Jesus sets the stage by telling the parable of the victimized Jew and the neighborly Samaritan.

Note that "it so happened" that a priest was going down the road from Jerusalem to Jericho when he came across the beaten man on the roadside. The impression is that the road is an isolated one, that the priest is returning to his home after service at the temple, and that he feared contracting ritual uncleanness by touching a dead body. In the same manner a Levite—not a priest but a cultic official with the role of overseeing rituals in the temple—passes by, perhaps also fearful about becoming ritually unclean. Such uncleanness was no small matter, since purification

could entail time-consuming and costly sacı
not see the priest and Levite as callous and
persons.

Along comes the Samaritan. Unbound b   ....
tions connected with religious practices, his heart is filled
with the kind of pity that moves him to action. He pours
oil and wine, healing liquids, on the beaten man's wounds,
then binds them. The Samaritan is selfless in his ministering. Not only does he stop and care for the man's injuries,
he also takes the Jewish victim to an inn, cares for him
there, then pays for more caring. As he leaves he pledges
to pay more on his way back. It is an example of the most
open-hearted generosity, an almost excessive compassion.
What the Samaritan did was more than anyone could expect. (Some see in this story an implicit reference to the
love Jesus has for humankind.) Moreover the Samaritans
were regarded by the Jews as bitter enemies, prime examples of those who would not be considered as neighbors
according to the Jewish understanding of Leviticus 19:18.
When Jesus asks the lawyer which man had acted like a
neighbor to the one attacked by robbers, the lawyer cannot
bring himself to say the word "Samaritan." He answers instead, "The one who was kind to him" (10:37).

Jesus has not only led the lawyer to answer his own
question, but he has also led the lawyer to reply in terms
he had never thought about. He did not receive a definition
of neighbor or a list of who was to be included and excluded in the category of neighbor. The answer came in
terms of what a neighbor does—namely, a neighbor acts
compassionately toward those who need compassion. Jesus' example of a neighbor goes beyond all boundaries of
race, religion, nationality or sex.

Finally, and here is one of the most beautiful Lucan insights into the meaning of Jesus' teaching, Jesus tells the

law_____ _____ 7). The law-
yer is given a mandate to be a neighbor to others. Thus Jesus has summed up the whole dialogue in a single
sentence, a dialogue that started with the lawyer's question, "What must I do to receive eternal life?"

REFLECTION. Many facets of the kingdom of God are
manifested in this parable. Note that the victim accepted
help from his enemy. The state of animosity that existed
between Jews and Samaritans was such that a Jew would
rather die than be helped by a Samaritan and a Samaritan
would prefer death to helping a Jew. In this parable Jesus
brings together two enemies in such a way as to provide a
glimpse of what the kingdom of God might be like—a situation in which enemies are reconciled on the basis of
helping and accepting help. It is not a situation in which
two equal parties work out an agreement based on mu-
tually beneficial effects. Perhaps the relationship between
Jew and Samaritan is an example of the kind of relationship
between persons and between nations that God intends to
exist when the kingdom comes in its fullness.

Jesus Visits Mary and Martha, 10:38–42

COMMENTARY. The wayfarer theme is again brought
out by Luke, who notes that Jesus and his disciples were
"on their way" (10:38). Luke is deliberately vague about
the location of Martha's home. We know from John 11:14
that Mary and Martha lived in Bethany on the outskirts of
Jerusalem. However, since Jesus has recently set out for Jerusalem (9:51), it is not yet time for Jesus to be ending his
journey. Luke leaves the village unnamed.
　Mary sits at the feet of the Lord and listens to her

Lord's teaching (10:39). Again this reveals Jesus' acceptance of women as the equals of men (see commentary on 8:1–3). Seated at the feet of Jesus, Mary is depicted as Jesus' disciple, listening to the teaching of her Master. In a society in which Jewish men prayed to God in thanksgiving for their not being born a Gentile, a slave or a woman, the position Mary assumes is one that challenges the social customs of the time.

Martha finds herself doing all the work for the preparation of the meal. She complains, expecting Jesus to tell Mary to get busy in the cooking area where she would seemingly belong. But Jesus gives Martha a startling reply: "Martha, Martha! . . . just one thing is needed" (10:41). While the "one thing" is subject to many interpretations, the episode itself provides us with the key to understanding this verse. Mary has been doing one thing: listening to Jesus. Martha, busy about the many details of preparing a meal for the guest, has not paid attention to her guest. Twice Jesus has to say her name—presumably to get Martha's attention. Jesus does not tell her to stop preparing the meal, but he does want her to attend to his presence. That is the one thing necessary. Mary, who sat at Jesus' feet and listened to him, "has chosen the right thing." Her discipleship will not be taken away from her. In this way Mary becomes the model of answering the implied question, "How do I love God?" One loves God by listening to Jesus and attending to his presence.

REFLECTION. Jesus' answer to Martha seems to look back to the explanation of the parable of the sower in 8:11–15. In the third group of unfruitful hearers are those who are choked by the worries of life (8:14). This is Martha's problem. She has so many cares—all legitimate, such as preparing a meal for a guest—that she does not have time to sit at Jesus' feet and allow his word to ripen within her and bear fruit.

The greatest difficulty of many Christians is the inability or refusal to choose the one thing needed. Jesus does not call us to give up our duties and responsibilities in this world. He does call us to go about our tasks without worry, trusting in the Father's loving care. In this way we can attend to Jesus (sit at his feet) at every moment and in every circumstance of life.

Jesus' Teaching on Prayer, 11:1–13

OVERVIEW. While Jesus and his disciples journey to Jerusalem, he teaches them how to pray. First Jesus responds to his followers' request by teaching them what we know as "the Lord's Prayer." Then he follows this with a parable that stresses the importance of persistent prayer (11:5–8). Finally, Jesus compares the readiness of God to answer the requests of his children with the loving responses of human fathers (11:11–13).

COMMENTARY. The context of Jesus' teaching is most significant. He is asked for instruction on prayer by his disciples, who want him to do for them what John did for his disciples (11:1). Thus the prayer taught by Jesus will express their identity as his followers just as the prayer of John's disciples demonstrated their communal identity. Jesus is about to share his experience of God—God as a loving Father—with his followers.

"Father" is the same address Jesus uses in his own prayer (see 10:21). The Hebrew Scriptures indicate that God was seen as a Father who deeply cared for Israel, his beloved child (see Dt 1:31; Hos 11:1; Is 49:15). Perhaps the stress on God's transcendence and the emphasis on the keeping of the Mosaic law lessened the sense of intimacy between God and his people. Whatever the reasons may have been, the way Jesus addressed God by the title *Abba* was amazingly revolutionary. Those who followed Jesus could well claim that their intimate and affectionate form of address, "Father," expressed much of their unique identity.

As the following comparison of the versions of Luke and Matthew indicate, there are differences. Matthew begins with "Our Father in heaven" whereas Luke simply has "Father." There are a variety of explanations as to why the versions differ. In general scholars suggest that the Lord's Prayer existed in two forms, and that rather than modifying the prayer as it was found in their sources, Luke and Matthew wrote the prayer as it was prayed in the liturgical celebrations of their communities.

Luke 11:1-4	**Matthew 6:8-13**
(1) One time Jesus was praying in a certain place. When he finished, one of his disciples said to him, "Lord, teach us to pray, just as John taught his disciples."	(7) "When you pray, do not use a lot of meaningless words, as the pagans do. . . .
	(8) "Do not be like them; your Father already knows what you need before you ask him.
(2) Jesus said to them, "This is what you should pray:	(9) This, then, is how you should pray:

'Father, may your holy name be honored;

'Our Father in heaven: May your holy name be honored;

may your Kingdom come.

(10) may your Kingdom come; may your will be done on earth as it is in heaven.

(3) Give us day by day the food we need.

(4) Forgive us our sins, because we forgive everyone who does us wrong.

(11) Give us today the food we need.

(12) Forgive us the wrongs that we have done, as we forgive the wrongs that others have done to us.

And do not bring us to hard testing.' "

(13) Do not bring us to hard testing, but keep us safe from the Evil One.' "

In the first petition "May your holy name be honored," the disciple asks God to bring about the situation in which his name is recognized by all. This petition has an end-time aspect in that the request can only be fully granted when the world is completely transformed. In the Semitic mentality, a name has a double function, both making present the one named and revealing his nature. Note the similarity with a petition in the Kaddish prayer which was said at the closing of the synagogue service: "May his name be glorified and honored as holy in the world, which he created according to his will."

The second petition, "May your Kingdom come," has a theme that parallels the first petition. The request for the kingdom asks the Father to bring about the full establishment of his reign. This request also looks to the end-time when the world will be finally transformed. This petition also has a parallel in the Kaddish: "May he establish his Kingdom in your lifetime and in your days and in all the ages of the whole house of Israel soon and in the near future."

The final three petitions of the prayer deal with the human needs of the disciples. The Greek words which are translated as "today" in Matthew and "day by day" in Luke's account have puzzled translators and scholars for centuries. Luke's phraseology expresses continuation in the giving and receiving of food. Here there may be a reference to the manna in the desert, which was given each day in the needed quantity (Ex 16:18). There is also the possibility that the food, as given by God, is a reference to the bread of the Eucharist. This interpretation would fit in with Luke's context of Jesus teaching a prayer that would express one's Christian identity. (In Matthew's account "daily food" can be translated as meaning "Give us today the bread of tomorrow," that is, the bread of the messianic banquet on the mountain where death will be destroyed forever; see Is 25:6–9. Since the Lord's Prayer looks toward the end-time, Jesus may have intended that we pray not only for bodily food but also for the food we will eat in the fellowship of the kingdom of God.)

The petition, "Forgive us our sins, because we forgive everyone who does us wrong," is the only portion of the Lord's Prayer in which the believer's action is mentioned (11:4). What we are called to do, namely, forgive those who do us wrong, is modeled upon the forgiveness of God.

God's forgiveness is total. In the prayer that expresses our identity as disciples of Jesus we ask that our sins would be forgiven in the very act of our forgiving others.

The fifth and final petition in Luke's version (Matthew has seven) asks that we be spared from trial. The phraseology of the *Today's English Version* translation is rather unfamiliar to us, but it means that we are asking the Father for the strength to withstand whatever might lead us away from him. The idea is this: we are praying that God will cause us not to yield to the doing of evil. If we interpret this petition from an end-time perspective, we might say that the Christian asks to be spared from the severe testing that will accompany the final days before the transformation of the world (see Lk 21:10–19).

The parable of the unwilling friend (11:5–9) is found only in Luke. Here we read about the way someone solves the problem of not having enough food on hand to provide hospitality for his newly arrived guest. The householder resolves his dilemma by going to a nearby friend and asking to borrow three loaves of bread. In the Greek text the phrase with which Jesus introduces this parable asks: "Can you imagine any one of you . . . ?" and the expected answer is a definitive "No"! Of course one could expect a friend to lend food to fulfill the heavy responsibility of providing hospitality for a guest. Verse 7 begins with a second "Can you imagine . . . " phrase. It would not be expected that a friend would refuse such a request simply because it would entail disturbing the sleeping family and opening the bars across the door. Jesus is saying that even if that unimaginable refusal was given, the one needing the bread would shamelessly continue to ask until his friend granted the request (11:8). The borrower has no shame because friendship is the basis which justifies his continued requesting. If such persistence in an earthly request is rewarded, how much more will God reward our persistence in seeking his gifts!

Verses 9 through 13 speak about the certainty of receiving from God's bounty, because prayer is a relationship between the disciple and his or her heavenly Father. God gives and God opens the doors we need opened. Note the element of joy present in one's praying to such a Father. If human parents, for all their sinfulness, rejoice in granting their children's requests, how much more will God attend to our requests (11:13)!

In the parallel passage found in Matthew the final sentence speaks of how much more the Father will "give good things to those who ask him" (Mt 7:11). In Luke's version Jesus speaks of the Father giving "the Holy Spirit to those who ask him" (11:13). The mention of the gift of the Holy Spirit sums up the teaching of Jesus in a most fitting way. Human fathers meet the needs of their children by providing for their bodily needs—a fish or an egg. Our heavenly Father gives what we need for life to the full—the presence of the same Spirit that gifted Mary (1:35), Elizabeth (1:41), Zechariah (1:67), Simeon (1:26) and Jesus (4:1, 18).

REFLECTION. It is the experience of every believer to have ardently prayed for that which is greatly desired—be that a request for a particular toy for Christmas or a successful surgery for one who is dearly loved—but which is not given. As a result some have concluded that prayers of petition are not worthy prayers. The teaching of Jesus proclaims just the opposite! Some others believe that God always answers our prayers, but his answer can be "Yes" or "No" or "Wait a while." Luke's version of Jesus' teaching that the Father grants the Holy Spirit to those who ask provides an occasion for us to deepen our appreciation of the prayer of petition. The Spirit is the greatest of all gifts. It is the Spirit who leads us to Jesus. In 1 Corinthians 12:3 Paul declares that the gift of the Spirit draws us into the very life of God, enabling us to name God as our Father and recognize our being related to him as sons and daughters in the Son. Luke will soon refer to the Spirit's being given to us when we need the right words to defend ourselves in time of trial and thereby bear witness to Jesus before governor and rulers (12:11–12). John tells us that the Spirit is "the Helper" who "will teach you everything and make you remember all that I have told you" (Jn 14:26).

When we pray, therefore, we can ask our Father for the gift of the Spirit who will help us to deal with loss, disappointment and tragedy. Strengthened by the Spirit, one can discern what can be done in the present and how one can find help in the community to bear the pain of the present. Even in our bitterest disappointments—and human life has many—we will find opportunity to enter more fully into our Father's loving care.

Week Five

During this portion of the Third Gospel the Pharisees challenge the authority of Jesus. They raise the question of what power is behind the cures done by the man from Nazareth. While attending a meal Jesus strongly criticizes the failings of the Pharisees and lawyers (11:37–54).

As the oppositon between Jesus and the religious leaders of Israel increases, Jesus addresses his disciples more directly. With parables and sayings Jesus urges his disciples to trust in God rather than riches, to profess their faith fearlessly, to be open-handed to those in need and to be ready at all times for the unexpected return of the Master (12:1–48).

Political opposition in the person of Herod manifests itself as Jesus draws closer to Jerusalem. Jesus continues to visit the homes of the Pharisees, speaking of the kingdom of God. Jesus tells the parable of the banquet which was enjoyed by those who were not originally invited. Chapter 14 concludes by pointing out some of the attitudes that should characterize the disciples of Jesus.

DAILY STUDY ASSIGNMENTS: WEEK FIVE

Day	Luke	Commentary
1	11:14–36	pp. 132–135
2	11:37—12:12	pp. 135–140
3	12:13–48	pp. 140–145
4	12:49—13:35	pp. 146–153
5	14:1–35	pp. 153–159

6 Review Luke 11:14—14:35 in light of the reflection questions at the end of this week's section.

7 Group meets for study and prayer.

1. What is at stake, that is, what is the issue involved in the request made of Jesus to perform a miracle to show that God approved of him (11:16)? What application can this episode have for your life?

2. In Luke 12:1–12 Jesus speaks of steadfast commitment in the face of persecution. What are some of the ways you have experienced opposition when you were trying to live as a follower of Jesus?

3. In the parable of the rich fool (12:13–21) Jesus warns us about placing our trust in things that make our human lives secure. How can the teaching of Jesus in this parable be applied to our own situation as we live in an economic system much different from that in first century Israel?

4. Jesus repeatedly asked his disciples to do away with worrying and to be concerned with God's kingdom

(12:22–31). What are your worries? What would happen if you let go of them? How can you understand and live out this teaching of Jesus?

5. In 13:34 Jesus laments because Jerusalem has rejected the prophets sent with God's message. Can you think of any instances in our history in which we Americans have rejected or killed prophetic figures? If yes, who were these messengers and how did their messages reflect the teachings of Jesus?

6. Jesus spoke of inviting the poor, the crippled, the lame and the blind to lunch or dinner (14:12–14). What application could this advice of Jesus have in our society? In our parishes?

Jesus and Beelzebul, 11:14–23

When Jesus cures a man unable to speak, the exorcism becomes an occasion for people to decide for or against Jesus. We can visualize the scene in terms of concentric circles, with Jesus at the center, his disciples gathered about him, and the amazed crowds standing in a circle around the disciples. The people in the crowd respond in different ways. Some of them allege (11:15) that Jesus is using power given to him by Beelzebul (literally meaning "Lord of the Flies"). Still others seek to trap Jesus by demanding a great sign (11:17). These did not consider an exorcism to be a sufficient indication of God's authorization of Jesus. (The demand for a miracle could be related to Jesus' third temptation in 4:9–12.)

The basic issue is not so much Jesus' ability to do powerful deeds. The issue deals with the ultimate source of Jesus' power. Those who did not accept Jesus' message explained their rejection of him by saying that the power of evil stands behind Jesus. Jesus replies by pointing out that it is not Satan who brings his own kingdom to ruin; it is the power of God that does this (11:18, 20)! In the actions of Jesus the kingdom of God is already operative. Jesus is the stronger man (11:22) that attacks and defeats the strong man (11:21). We can see in the deliverance of the speechless man (11:14) the proof that the kingdom of God has drawn near. For this reason Jesus declares that there can be no neutrality. One is either for Jesus and God's reign, or one is against him as he labors to gather the people for "the owner of the harvest" (11:23 and 10:2).

The Return of the Evil Spirit, 11:24–26

Luke follows the controversy over the meaning of Jesus' exorcism with a parable demonstrating the importance of continued commitment. If a person has been exorcised but does not act to replace the evil with good, that emptiness invites disaster. Because the person in the parable displays no proof of conversion, the original demon returns and, reinforced by seven others (seven being the number that symbolizes fullness), retakes possession of the man. Thus he ends up worse than before because the eight evil spirits will be able to strongly resist future attempts at exorcism (11:26).

True Happiness, 11:27–28

These verses are found only in Luke. We have seen that Jesus has been speaking to crowds of people who were amazed when Jesus exorcised the man who could not speak (11:14). Jesus then demonstrated how his signs revealed that the power of God is with him as he goes about defeating the strong man and releasing the stolen goods (11:20–22). A woman responds to Jesus' teaching by praising Jesus' mother, declaring that she is blessed in bearing such a son as Jesus. Perhaps the implication is that the woman is saying how happy she would be to have a son like Jesus! Jesus, however, shifts the focus of the woman's remark by strongly declaring that the real source of happiness comes from the obedient hearing of the word of God (11:28). It is a remarkable message for the woman, for it proclaims to her that she can take her place beside his mother and disciples, for they have already heard the word of God and are living it out (see 8:21).

The Demand for a Miracle, 11:29–32

The Good News Bible fails to bring out the idea that the crowds around Jesus are increasing (11:29). As more people have arrived, Jesus develops his answer to those who had asked for a sign (see 11:16). In this instance Jesus qualifies his refusal to perform a miracle: the evil people of this day (a reference to those who will not believe unless they are awed by demonstrations of power) shall be given "the miracle of Jonah." While Matthew's account speaks of the sign of Jonah in terms of Jesus' resurrection (three days in the whale's belly, three days in the earth—Mt 12:39–40), Luke develops the thought that the sign of Jonah is the fact that the people of Nineveh repented after hearing the prophet's warning. God had sent his prophet to the pagans and they accepted his message. We see a similar theme in Jesus' inaugural discourse in Nazareth. There Jesus had spoken of God sending Elijah and Elisha to aid the Gentiles (4:25–27).

The queen of Sheba is only remotely related to the sign of Jonah. As Jonah traveled far to deliver his message to the pagans, the queen of the South traveled far to hear the wisdom of Solomon. In contrast to both Jonah and the queen, the Son of Man is already in the midst of his people, but they refuse to hear and repent even though someone far greater than either Jonah or Solomon is present (11:32).

The Light of the Body, 11:33–35

Luke brings closure to Jesus' teaching on the relationship between signs and faith by collecting several sayings that deal with light. The light that is put on a stand in order to illuminate the house conveys the idea that Jesus is a light given by God and that his message is not so obscure as to need miracles to demonstrate its validity.

In the second metaphor we find a teaching on spiritual vision and spiritual blindness. If the light of the Gospel penetrates one's eyes, then one's whole body is filled with light. Just as one's life is shrouded in darkness when one is blind, so too, one's existence is spent in darkness without the illumination of Jesus' teaching (11:36).

Jesus Criticizes the Pharisees and the Teachers of the Law, 11:37–51

Luke changes the scene by shifting from Jesus' public discourse to a meal at the home of a Pharisee. As we have seen in 7:36 and will see in 14:1, Luke uses the setting of a meal with a Pharisee when Jesus is about to give some interpretation regarding the law and the Pharisaic traditions that were meant to protect the law, i.e., see that the Mosaic law was observed to the full. Many of the teachings of Jesus on this occasion are also found in Matthew 23:1–39.

When the Pharisee expresses surprise at Jesus' eating without washing, Jesus seizes the occasion to point out the difference between external appearances and interior dispositions. What follows is a searing critique on those who appear outwardly religious while inwardly lacking those dispositions that make religious practices truly authentic. Just as the cleansing of the outside of a dirty vessel without washing the inside as well amounts to foolishness, so religion based on externals without concern for one's inner attitude is foolish and reprehensible. The reference to interior violence and evil, in light of Jesus' admonition to give what is in their cups and plates to the poor, suggests that greed may motivate some of the Pharisees. Jesus may also be referring to the need to share one's goods with the poor in order to truly cleanse the heart and be in solidarity with the poor and lowly whom God regards with loving concern (see 1:50–55).

In verses 42 through 44 Jesus pronounces three denunciations of those Pharisees whose religious practices show more concern for outer appearance than inner dispositions. (It is important to realize that Pharisees were laymen who studied the Mosaic law with the intention of knowing and doing the will of God. While some did fall into the pitfall of giving priority to external actions, not all Pharisees did so.) The denunciations "How terrible for you . . ." are not curses calling down God's anger upon the Pharisees and lawyers. They are lamentations, for they express grief about a situation in which God's people are led by such spiritual guides as those who are meticulous about giving God a tenth of their garden herbs while ignoring their responsibility to live lovingly and justly (11:42). Jesus' second lament deals with the yielding of some Pharisees to the temptation of seeking public acclaim for what they do (11:43). The third lament represents a scathing criticism of the spiritual leaders of Israel. By comparing them with unmarked graves (11:44), Jesus is saying that they are contaminating the people they seek to serve. While their outward behavior is proper (they don't have the appearance of graves), underneath they are filled with corruption (the decay within the graves).

Verse 45 provides the transition from Jesus' lamentations regarding the Pharisees to three laments directed at the teachers of the law (11:46, 52) and others (11:47–51). Jesus finds fault with the teachers of the law not only because they load their legalities on the backs of the people, but also because they lack any concern for helping the people to observe them. The crux of Jesus' criticism is that they lack love for those they should be serving. The lawyers lay down the law and merely demand that others live it out, while they can use their knowledge of legalities to spare themselves from the law's burdens. In today's terminology it could be said that the lawyers had no "pastoral concern" for the ordinary people.

The second lamentation in this section is directed at a wider group than the teachers of the law. It was the fashion in Jesus' day to make elaborate graves for honored persons. The line of reasoning in verses 47 through 51 is difficult to follow. It seems that Jesus is saying that only after God's prophets are persecuted and killed do they receive the respect that is their due. Jesus accuses his contemporaries of being like their ancestors, because they also refuse to hear the prophets who call them to conversion. For this reason the people of Jesus' own day will find themselves judged and punished (11:50–51). This saying probably anticipates the destruction of Jerusalem in 70 A.D.

In the final lamentation the teachers of the law are found blameworthy for having the key of learning that opens the door to knowledge of God while refusing to use that key to enter. Their guilt is all the more because they, the religious leaders of Israel, use their position to prevent God's people from a deeper appreciation of God and his kingdom (11:52).

In verse 53, appearing only in Luke, we learn about the process in which the oppositon to Jesus develops. Lawyers and Pharisees begin a twofold process of criticism and of attempts to discredit his teaching authority by catching him in some kind of contradiction. The scribes and Pharisees are not depicted as wanting to kill Jesus. If they cannot make him their disciple, which they seem to want to do by their practice of inviting him to eat with them in their homes (see 7:36; 11:37 and 14:1), then they will try to stop the movement Jesus has started by discrediting its leader.

Instructions and Warnings, 12:1—13:9

OVERVIEW. In this long section Luke draws from the Q document and his own special source. Jesus continues to teach publicly, but his instructions are mainly directed to his disciples (see 12:1, 4, 22, 32). At the same time, however, the crowds are in the background (12:1). Jesus also interacts with the crowd (12:13) and addresses the crowds directly (12:54). Much of the material that Luke includes in 12:1—13:9 is found also in Matthew but divided between three of Jesus' long discourses. Perhaps Luke has gathered the instructions of Jesus here for catechetical purposes. In this long section Jesus constantly reminds his disciples about their priorities: they are to profess their faith in Jesus without fear (12:1–12), be wary of the danger of riches (12:13–34), be always ready for their Master's return (12:35–48), and be prepared to face persecution (12:49–54).

A Warning Against Hypocrisy, 12:1–3

COMMENTARY. The thousands of people surrounding Jesus and his disciples represent the movement the Pharisees are determined to stop by laying traps for Jesus (11:53). Jesus refers to his criticisms of the Pharisees and lawyers (11:39–52) as he urges his disciples to fearlessly proclaim the good news. No matter what the circumstances, the disciple of Jesus is called to be a witness of Jesus and his teachings. The mysteries of the kingdom of God, at first understood interiorly, must be lived out publicly. The follower of Jesus is to proclaim from housetops (the traditional place from which public announcements were made in the Jewish towns) the Gospel they have received from Jesus (12:3).

Whom To Fear, 12:4–7

The "friends" Jesus addresses are those close to him, his disciples. He tells them in the starkest of words that they are to be fearless in the face of death. Some of their enemies may have the power to take away their earthly lives, but bodily death is preferable to the loss of everlasting life (12:5).

Having stated that the fear of God can help his disciples overcome the fear of other people, Jesus then speaks of God as the one who cares for them with the greatest solicitude (12:7). God, who is revealed by Jesus as *Abba*, Father (11:2), cares even for the sparrow. Jesus concludes his warning with words of encouragement: "So do not be afraid; you are worth much more than many sparrows!"

On Professing and Rejecting
the Son of Man, 12:8–12

The verses dealing with publicly professing or denying one's commitment to Jesus (12:8–9) parallel the thought in 12:4. There may be great risk in letting one's discipleship with Jesus be known, but greater risk is entailed by not doing so. Then Jesus will not know them as his disciples when judgment day comes (12:9).

However, even if the disciple does yield to the fear of others and thereby denies Jesus by speaking against the Son of Man, forgiveness is always possible (12:10a). The one exception to the giving of forgiveness is the instance of speaking against the Holy Spirit (12:10b). While the God of mercy never withdraws his merciful love, there is one situation in which a person can use his or her freedom to reject God. That one situation is to look on the works of light and declare them to be the works of darkness.

In the next two verses Jesus gives further encouragement to his disciples. Jesus had taught them that their Father would always hear their prayers and give them the Holy Spirit (11:13). Now Jesus reassures them that when persecution comes, the Holy Spirit will inspire them with what they need to say in their defense (12:12). As we know from Luke's second work, the Acts of the Apostles, he was familiar with the way the followers of Jesus suffered at the hands of their Jewish brethren. In the decades after the death and resurrection of Jesus, particularly after the destruction of the temple by the Romans in 70 A.D., those Jews who accepted Jesus as the Messiah had come to be regarded as heretics by the guardians of official Judaism. Those who were followers of "the Way" were subject to harassment, beatings and arrest by civil authorities (see Acts 12:5; 14:19–20; 24:22–23). Luke here reminds his audiences in the various local churches to remain steadfast in their faith by placing before them the words of Jesus about reliance on the power of God's Spirit.

The Parable of the Rich Fool, 12:13–21

This parable stands at the beginning of a section which deals with the attitude of disciples regarding earthly possessions (12:13–34). Someone in the crowd, recognizing the air of authority in Jesus, asks Jesus to be the arbiter in a property dispute with his brother. Jesus declines but uses the incident to warn his audience about the danger of acquiring possessions. The danger of riches is a key theme in Luke's account of the Gospel. There is an element of mystery involved, a search for the right balance between poverty and possessing the goods of creation. While material things are good, the desire to possess them can lead to sin. In this parable of the wealthy farmer, found only in Luke, Jesus speaks of the personal consequences of seeking security in possessions. To place property above all other considerations is to close oneself off from God—that is the point Jesus makes in telling the story about the rich fool.

The man in the parable has such an abundance of goods that his one concern is to build bigger barns to house his growing wealth. Instead of praying, he carries on a monologue with himself: "And I will say to myself, Lucky man! You have all the good things you need for many years. Take life easy, eat, drink, and enjoy yourself!" That very night God declared "You fool!" and called the man to judgment (12:20). Jesus concluded: "This is how it is with those who pile up riches for themselves but are not rich in God's sight" (12:21). The man's disastrous mistake was to neglect the source of his "true life" (12:15). Having ignored both God and neighbor, the rich man was lacking what really mattered in the sight of God. He had the easy life on earth. In death his time for sorrow begins. This parable echoes the woes Jesus pronounced in his Sermon on the Plain:

> But how terrible for you who are rich now; you have had your easy life! How terrible for you who are full now; you will go hungry! How terrible for you who laugh now; you will mourn and weep! (6:24–25).

REFLECTION. Because of the differences between our complex economic system and the simpler economy of the first century, it may be difficult for us to grasp the full import of 12:15–21. It would miss the point to conclude that Jesus is against bank accounts or protecting one's investments. It would also miss the point to say that the modern disciples of Jesus should not purchase insurance policies on health or home because these will undermine our trust in God. What is at stake is the recognition that there *is* a particular attitude toward investments and insurance policies that does lead us away from God; it is the conviction that having these will provide us with all the security we need. Jesus warns us all: "Watch out and guard yourselves from every kind of greed; because a person's true life is not made up of the things he owns . . ." (12:15).

Trusting in God, 12:22–34

Luke follows the parable of the rich man with some of the sayings of Jesus (drawn from the Q source) in order to indicate the proper attitude of the disciple. The crux of Jesus' teaching is this: trust in God your Father.

In verses 22–34, one of the most familiar passages in the New Testament, Jesus declares four times that his disciples should not worry or be upset (12:22, 25 and 29). Jesus does not call us to leave our human condition; we will always need food, drink and clothing. The key that opens the full meaning of this passage is verse 31: by trusting in the Father's providential care, the believer becomes free to devote his or her primary concern to the kingdom (God's reign in human history). In the prayer that identifies the disciples of Jesus we were taught to pray, "Father: may . . . your Kingdom come. Give us day by day the food we need" (11:2–3). When Jesus speaks of the birds of the air and the wild flowers, he is reminding us that we are always, like the whole of creation, in the presence of God.

In verse 32 Jesus addresses his disciples by the title "little flock." Indeed, Jesus' original band of disciples as well as his followers in the local churches of the 80's, scattered here and there about the eastern portion of the Roman Empire, would find the term an apt description of themselves and their vulnerable situation. Jesus asks them not to fear because it is to them, the poor and lowly of the world, that God desires to give his kingdom (12:32). The universal Church, the totality of all disciples, is most itself when it is most powerless. Then the community realizes that it does not create the kingdom; the community accepts the kingdom as God's gift. The admonition to sell all belongings and give them to the poor expresses what should be the basic attitude of all disciples: open-handed giving. In Luke's ideal portrayal of Christian community we see Jesus' followers sharing all their belongings:

> *All the believers continued together in close fellowship and shared their belongings with one another. They would sell their property and possessions, and distributed the money among all, according to what each one needed (Acts 2:44–45).*

The admonition to provide "purses that don't wear out" and to save one's riches for heaven further illuminates the meaning of the parable of the rich barn builder. By piling up riches for himself, he lost the chance to be "rich in God's sight" (12:21). In verse 33 we are told that sharing our belongings with the poor makes us rich in heaven, that is, rich in God's sight. Verse 34 sums up the entire section. The "heart" in Scripture refers to the inner core of the person. If we "set our heart" on trivial and passing "riches" we trivialize our very personhood. Yet if we set our hearts on God's kingdom, we store up treasure for eternity.

On Being Prepared for the
Master's Return, 12:35–48

OVERVIEW. Jesus' instruction of his disciples (see 12:22) continues, but the subject matter shifts from attitudes toward possessions to the idea of always being ready for the return of the Son of Man. This section includes four parables: the wedding feast (12:35–38), the thief in the night (12:39–40), the faithful and unfaithful servants (12:42–46), and the two servants (12:47–48). The first three parables are found, at least in part, in Matthew.

COMMENTARY. When Jesus first told these parables, he was asking his audience to make a decision for the kingdom of God. Jesus urged his listeners to turn to God so that they would be ready to celebrate the messianic wedding banquet when God's kingdom broke into human history (12:36–38). That moment would come suddenly and unexpectedly, like a thief (12:39).

In the early decades of the Church's history there was the expectation that Jesus would soon return in glory. As the delay of Jesus' second coming grew longer, some Christians were tempted to give up their faith in Jesus; others became complacent about the way they lived, having neither great faith nor high expectations. So, the community reworked some of the parables of Jesus, adapting them to the needs of the believing communities by stressing the theme of being ready for Jesus at whatever time he did come back. Thus the emphasis on making a decision now for the kingdom of God shifted to a stress on being ready and vigilant for Jesus' return at all times. Jesus, having ascended to the Father, is already at the wedding feast. No one knows when he will return to bring his disciples into the fullness of the kingdom. He may come at midnight or even later (12:38). The important aspect in both the parable of the servants waiting for their master and the example of the homeowner is this: "You, too, must be ready, because the Son of Man will come at any hour when you are not expecting him" (12:40). The disciples who are ready to welcome their Master will receive an astonishing reward. The Master himself will become their "servant" and wait on their table (12:37). How happy, indeed, they will be!

Peter's question (12:41), found only in Luke, serves to indicate that Jesus' teaching regarding watchfulness was not only intended for the original apostles, but also for all disciples, including those Gentiles who would become Jesus' disciples in the future. Jesus' response in 12:42–48 means that those disciples in leadership positions were to be faithful and vigilant in proportion to their greater responsibility for the community. Thus, the "faithful and wise servant" Jesus refers to (12:42) can be seen as a symbol of the Christian leader, the one in charge of the other servants. Because he provides for their needs, he will be happy when his Master comes and finds him ministering as he ought (12:43).

In contrast, the unfaithful servant neglects and mistreats the servants in his care, while indulging himself with food and drink. This servant symbolizes the disciple who thinks that the delay of Jesus' coming may mean that Jesus will not come at all (12:45). To this servant's dismay, the Master returns unexpectedly. The unfaithful servant is cut off. His sharing in the "fate of the disobedient" (12:46) connects with the fate of those who heard the words of Jesus but did not obey them. Like the householder who did not build on a foundation (6:49), the disobedient servant regretfully finds his future in ruins.

Jesus, the Cause of Division, 12:49–53

In a certain sense "history repeats itself." Eight centuries before Jesus lived, the prophet Micah deplored Israel's loss of values: "In these times sons treat their fathers like fools, daughters oppose their mothers . . . a man's enemies are the members of his own family" (Mic 7:6). Jesus was calling his people to a new allegiance—to God and to his own teachings. Jesus also realized that those who followed him as his disciples would find themselves in conflict with those relatives who did not accept his message and life-style. One of the areas of conflict concerned the clash in messianic expectations on the part of many of the first-century Jews. Because of the harshness of the Roman occupation, it was difficult for the Jewish people to see where true zeal for Yahweh's chosen people ended and where self-inflating nationalism began. We can imagine that many people, hoping for the day when a nationalistic Messiah would restore Israel to the status it had under the powerful King David, were not open to Jesus' message of non-violent living, forgiveness, love of one's enemy, and inner freedom in the service of God. Thus, households were divided between those who accepted the teachings of Jesus and those who did not.

Jesus Summons All to Repentance 12:54–13:9

In verses 35 to 48 we have seen how Luke took four parables in which Jesus had challenged Israel to repent and adapted them to the situation of Jesus' delayed return to earth. Although these four parables had some particular application to the leaders of the believing communities, the main theme of these parables is less concerned with the imminent return of Jesus and more concerned with the community's being prepared for his coming at any time—even in the distant future. Now, in verse 54, Jesus addresses the crowds, warning them of the implications of what he had said to his disciples about being ready at all times. The crowds ought to be able to read "the meaning of present time" (12:56), that is, they ought to see that they are being addressed by God through the preaching of Jesus. If they can predict the weather, they are nothing more than hypocrites if they cannot see the power of God at work in Jesus.

Thus Jesus challenges his audience to do the right thing (12:57). They are already being led to judgment. However, they can settle with their opponent before they arrive at court. There is still time to accept Jesus and his message. But when judgment day comes, the time for reconciliation will be past. Therefore, use the opportunity to repent now, while they are still on their earthly journey. Death will destroy that opportunity, and then each one will have to pay the full consequence of his or her refusal to repent (12:59).

In 13:1–9 Luke includes material from his own unique source. In the crowd are some persons who have either just arrived with news of Pilate's latest atrocity or who are responding to Jesus' words regarding judgment. They relate the story of the victims in a way that suggests the victims were under God's judgment. Jesus responds to their presumed innocence by challenging both the self-appointed messengers and his audience to see what is really at issue: the call to repent. The Galileans killed by Pilate and the eighteen men killed in the accident in Siloam were no better or no worse than the rest of the people in his audience. Judgment will fall on all sinners, including Jesus' listeners—unless they repent (13:5).

The call to repentance is immediately followed by a

parable that reveals the merciful patience of God (13:6–9).
The barren tree symbolizes Israel which lacks the fruits of
repentance. Perhaps the three year period in which the
owner (God) of the tree has looked for figs is a reference to
Jesus' ministry (13:7). The gardener pleads for more time,
and thus judgment is delayed by a merciful reprieve. However, if the people of Israel continue to lack the fruits of repentance, then the axe of judgment will come for certain
(13:9). In the meantime the continued ministry of Jesus is
a time of grace offered to Israel. No one, Jew or Gentile,
should take God's patience for granted (see 12:57–59).

Jesus Heals a Woman on the Sabbath, 13:10–17

Early in his ministry, prior to choosing the twelve, Jesus taught in a synagogue and cured a man who had a
paralyzed hand (6:6–11). This healing took place on a sabbath and led some religious leaders to oppose Jesus. Now,
on the way to Jerusalem, Jesus again teaches in a synagogue (13:10), but for the last time. Jesus notices the crippled woman, then takes the initiative. Calling her forward,
Jesus declares her free of her sickness as he lays his hands
upon her. Cured immediately, she praises God (13:13). Notice how the ruler of the synagogue responds in an entirely
different way. Angrily he indirectly rebukes Jesus by declaring to the people that six days of the week are reserved
for work while the sabbath is not (13:19). At issue is the
interpretation of the healing. The leader of the synagogue
saw Jesus' laying on of hands to cure the woman as an act
of human work; he failed to see God's hand in the liberation of a woman from an infirmity that had kept her bent
over for eighteen years. Then Jesus replies, pointing out
the great difference between what the religious leaders

permit and forbid on the sabbath. If it is permitted to do the work of untying a knot in order to spare an animal from thirst on the sabbath, then how much more it should be permitted to release a Jewish woman from eighteen years of physical bondage!

Satan is referred to as the one who kept the woman in bondage, because in him the power of evil was personified. The people of Jesus' day attributed to Satan the leading of people astray, inciting them to oppose God and inflicting them with mental and physical disorders. The meaning of Jesus' cure of the woman is this: even now the kingdom of evil is losing ground; already it is on its way to ultimate and utter defeat. The people rejoiced because they, unlike the ruler of the synagogue, could view this healing as a prelude to the ultimate victory of God.

Two Parables About the Kingdom, 13:18–21

Appropriately enough, the account of the healing of the crippled woman is followed by two parables about the kingdom of God. Both parables contrast the tiny beginnings of God's reign with its future maturity. The small mustard seed, proverbially the smallest seed, grows into a tree vastly out of proportion with what might be expected in terms of its initial size. Often reaching a height of twelve feet, the mustard tree becomes large enough to provide a home for birds. The lesson of the parable is found in the potential of the seed that symbolizes the kingdom. In spite of such a tiny beginning, the kingdom's potential is enormous.

For a second time Jesus seeks something from the realm of his listeners' experience with which to compare the kingdom's potential for growth (13:20). He chooses the effect that a small amount of yeast has in transforming the whole batch of dough. The growth taking place in the dough is silent and secret but in the end the yield of bread from a bushel of flour is huge.

REFLECTION. We may well think of the Church as the yeast in society that brings about the transformation of the world. In the episode that precedes the two parables about the tiny beginnings of the kingdom, a woman crippled for eighteen years is released from her infirmity. The evidence for the defeat of evil is slight in comparison with the number of persons suffering from physical illness or from the dehumanizing effects of poverty, political oppression or racism. However, this one instance of the defeat of the forces of evil, small as it is, is a sign of the coming of God's kingdom. Jesus is teaching his disciples that they must not become impatient with the slow, silent growth of the reign of God. We are the twentieth century disciples of Jesus. How good it is to be part of the growth of the kingdom, for it will inevitably reach its full and glorious maturity. It is also our privilege to impart this good news to the young members of the believing community. The bishops of the Second Vatican Council spoke of our privilege in these words:

> We can justly consider that the future of humanity lies in the hands of those who are strong enough to provide coming generations with reasons for living and hoping (Pastoral Constitution on the Church in the Modern World, #31).

The Narrow Door, Unrepentant Jews, Believing Gentiles, 13:22–30

COMMENTARY. Jesus has taught in a synagogue for the last time (13:10–17). He continues to make his way to Jerusalem while teaching in those towns and villages through which he journeys (13:22). In response to a question about the number of those to be saved, Jesus uses the metaphor of the narrow door to illustrate the necessity of repenting while there is still time to do so. There are two basic ideas here. First, one's time for conversion will not last forever; therefore go through the narrow door of repentance before that door is shut. The second idea is the insufficiency of merely hearing the message of Jesus. Table fellowship with Jesus, the fact that one ate and drank with him, will not be enough to save a person. The narrow door is entered by conversion; once shut, the unrepentant will find themselves on the wrong side. Since they failed to live out his teachings, Jesus will not acknowledge them (13:27; see 6:49). Thus those who refused to take the call to repentance to heart find themselves excluded from the presence of Abraham and the prophets in the kingdom. The Gentiles, those who respond to Jesus from the four directions of the compass, will be included in the heritage of God's people (see Is 2:1–5), while some of Abraham's descendants will find themselves weeping and gnashing their teeth in despair (13:28–29). The saying about the first and the last is a proverb that had many applications. The theme of reversal probably refers to the Jews, the first to hear the good news but not accepting it, and the Gentiles, who heard the Gospel last but yet embraced it and found salvation (13:30).

Jesus Warned About Herod, 13:31–33

Since Luke notes that it was "at that same time" (13:31) as Jesus was preaching repentance that "some Pharisees" came to Jesus with a warning about Herod, it is likely that the evangelist wants his readers to connect the two scenes. Herod, an unjust ruler who has murdered John the Baptist, may have had intentions to end the life of Jesus. It is not clear what the motives of the Pharisees are in this case. They may have been genuinely interested in Jesus' welfare or they may have been interested in diverting Jesus from his mission of healing, exorcising and calling people to repentance. The answer of Jesus, "Go and tell that fox," indicates that Jesus may have regarded these Pharisees as emissaries of Herod himself (13:32). Since the fox often symbolized mean cunning, Jesus indicated that he was not looking for any kind of appeasement. His words carry the conviction of a person determined to follow his conscience while trusting in God that he would accomplish his work or purpose. The assertion that his work will be completed on the third day and the statement that the prophet cannot die except in Jerusalem seem to point to Jesus' death and resurrection (13:32–33).

Jesus Laments for Jerusalem, 13:34–35

These two verses look ahead to Jesus' arrival in Jerusalem and his preaching ministry there. Through his whole ministry he has been asking his people to turn back to God. Jesus' preaching in the holy city will be their final chance. If they would only listen to him, disaster would be averted. The winds of the Jewish-Roman War (66–73 A.D.) have already begun to blow (see 19:41–44). Having set his face like stone toward Jerusalem (9:51), Jesus will journey there in spite of the past fate of God's prophets (13:34).

The images Jesus uses are drawn from the Hebrew Scriptures which compared God's affection for his people with that of a mother for her child (see Is 49:15) or of a bird sheltering her young (see Dt 32:11; Pss 17:8; 36:7). The reference to the abandonment of the temple (13:35) may be seen as God's departing the city after being rejected by his people. In verse 35 there are echoes of earlier prophetic pronouncements in which Yahweh is depicted as leaving the temple (Jer 12:7; Ez 10:18–19). The words of Jesus in 13:35 could refer to his triumphal entrance into Jerusalem (see 19:38) or it could refer to his coming as Judge at the end time.

Healing and Teaching During a Sabbath Banquet, 14:1–24

OVERVIEW. In the context of a sabbath meal, probably following a synagogue service, Luke presents Jesus as continuing his healing and teaching ministry in spite of increasingly hostile opposition. There are four sections to this episode in the home of a leading Pharisee. The first involves the healing of a man suffering from dropsy (14:2–6); the second section (14:7–11) deals with Jesus' observations about table manners and applications to the meaning of the kingdom; the third section (14:12–14) conveys Jesus' advice for his host regarding the invitation of particular guests; in the fourth unit Jesus tells a parable which illustrates the urgency of accepting the invitation to repent (14:15–24). These four sections carry forward the themes found in 13:22–30; the identity of those who will be saved by entering the kingdom (13:22–27) and the movement of the kingdom away from those who had been first called toward those who did not belong to the family of Abraham (13:28–30).

COMMENTARY. The setting for 14:1–24 is the home of an important Pharisee. This episode is sometimes referred to as the "Lukan symposium" because Luke has apparently collected snatches of Jesus' "table talk" and placed his words in the context of a sabbath banquet. We can imagine groups of guests standing about prior to taking their places at the table. Some guests are keeping a watchful eye on the teacher and healer from Nazareth as he is approached by a man suffering from dropsy (14:1). In a scene similar to that recounted in 6:6–11, Jesus confronts those who are specialists in the Mosaic law. He takes the initiative and asks: "Does our Law allow healing on the Sabbath or not?" At stake is the issue of the permissibility of doing a work of healing on the sabbath. The lawyers and teachers remain silent as Jesus heals the sick man. Then Jesus, a teacher himself, gives his own interpretation of the law in the form of a question regarding the emergency situation in which a son or ox had fallen into a well (14:5). Even on a sabbath would not the religious leaders work to pull out the child or animal? Jesus uses here the rabbinic principle of light matter versus heavy matter. This principle enabled a teacher of the law to take a principle that applied in a lesser case and then apply it to a more important case. The implication of Jesus' act of healing is that if it is lawful to do the work required to pull a child or beast from a well on the sabbath, then it is lawful to heal on the sabbath. The episode concludes with the observation that the Pharisees and teachers of the law could not answer Jesus, that is, they could not refute his interpretation.

When the time for taking places at the table came, the guests were competing for the best places. Jesus used the occasion to speak about the nature of the kingdom of God (14:7–11). The "wedding feast" (14:8) is a symbol of the kingdom of God; the host represents God. Placement at the table in the kingdom depends on one's recognition of his or her dependence upon God. Those who presume they are worthy of high places in the kingdom, such as the religious elite of Israel, will find themselves very surprised as they are asked to take a lower place. Jesus points out that those who recognize their lowliness in not having any claim or right to salvation will find themselves raised up to the highest places. This is another instance of the "reversal" theme that recurs throughout the Third Gospel. The reversal of the places of the powerful and the lowly is most clearly expressed in Mary's canticle, particularly in 1:52.

Verses 12 to 14 restate the themes found in 6:32–35 of the Sermon on the Plain. In the context of the sabbath banquet Jesus emphasizes the importance of generosity for the poor and disadvantaged. In words directly addressed to the host Jesus points out that if one person has the resources to provide banquets, then friendship, family relationship and social status should not be the only criteria for sharing those resources with others. It would be better for the host to invite the poor, the crippled, the lame and the blind, because this kind of selfless sharing is indeed a sign that one will participate in the resurrection of the just (14:13–14). Jesus is not advocating that one should never celebrate with friends and relatives. He himself did so, for example, at the home of Martha (10:38–42) and at the Passover seder (22:14–23). Perhaps the seemingly unworthy and undeserving poor, lame and blind persons will be the very people who will be told to go up higher at the wedding banquet in the kingdom (14:10).

The remark made by one of Jesus' hearers, "How happy are those who will sit down at the feast in the Kingdom of God!" serves as an opportunity for Jesus to introduce another parable about the kingdom. To appreciate this parable more fully, bear in mind that for large banquets two invitations were issued. The first requested the recipient's presence at an event that would take place in the weeks to come. Then, at a later date, when calves were fattened and all was in readiness, a second invitation was sent out regarding the exact day for the festivities. With knowledge of this procedure, the deeper significance of the parable is more readily seen. The man who is about to give the great feast is God; he sends out the first invitation (14:16). Since the people invited in this general invitation had already accepted, their refusal to come when told that all is ready (14:17) is rudely inconsiderate. The excuses they offer (14:18–20) are expressions of their individualist preoccupations—all of which should have been postponed in the light of the invitations they had already accepted. There could be a connection between this parable and the explanation of the parable of the sower, in which "the worries and riches and pleasures of this life" are the thorn bushes that choke the seedlings so that "their fruit never ripens" (8:14).

The Master is furious when he learns that his second invitation has been rejected (14:21). He sends his servant to go into the town to invite the outcasts, the poor, crippled and blind (14:21), the very ones Jesus had suggested that his host would do well to invite to his banquets (14:13). When there is still room after the arrival of the poor and disabled, the Master sends his servants to the country roads. In this way distant persons, symbolizing the Gentiles, are invited to the banquet. It is the end-time banquet to which God first invited the Jewish people. Now that invitation is extended to the Gentiles so that the Master's house will be filled (14:23). The conclusion (14:24) echoes the outcome of the parable on the narrow door: "Then those who are now last will be first, and those who are now first will be last" (13:30).

The Cost of Being a Disciple, 14:25–35

Luke's arrangement of Jesus' words on discipleship are an appropriate follow-through on the parable of the great supper. We have seen that the excuses given for not coming to the banquet dealt with business and domestic concerns (14:18–20). Throughout the Third Gospel Jesus continually points to the ways that possessions and worldly concerns distract people from hearing the call to discipleship (see 9:57–62). In this section Luke gathers together the sayings of Jesus that stress how important it is to realize fully what discipleship calls for. We are not to underestimate what total commitment to Jesus entails. As Jesus concludes, it calls for everything: "None of you can be my disciple unless he gives up everything he has" (14:33).

The context of Jesus' teaching sets the stage for what he will say. Great crowds of people were going with him (14:25). To "go with" Jesus is an expression of discipleship. Keep in mind that Jesus is on his way to Jerusalem, the city that kills the prophets (13:34). Jesus tells these potential disciples that they will have to be ready not only to leave behind family (14:26) but also to carry the cross after him (14:27) if they are to in fact be his followers. If father, mother, spouse or any other member of one's family would interfere with one's discipleship, then the disciple would have to leave one's family behind. In the first century context of persecution and pressure from family members who were not believers, those who followed Jesus sometimes had to make this difficult choice.

We have seen the teaching of Jesus regarding the taking up of one's cross in 9:23. Behind the image of taking up the cross is an attitude of total renunciation. Anyone who had to "take up" the cross was already condemned to die; thus one's life in this world is in effect already ended. From

that point onward a person must live in another way. It is
as Paul expressed it:

> *His death was death to sin, once for all; his life is life for God.*
> *In the same way, you must consider yourselves dead to sin*
> *but alive for God in Christ Jesus (Rom 6:10–11, NAB).*

Since Jesus asks his followers for such complete self-
renunciation, he wants them to consider seriously what is
at stake in being his disciple. Hence Jesus tells two parables
in which the main character has to carefully consider his
ability to complete a particular undertaking. In the first
story the builder must calculate the costs of building a
tower lest he not have enough funds to complete the proj-
ect (14:28–30). In the second parable a king must carefully
weigh his chances of success in battle before going out to
meet his foe (14:31–32). The second parable more strongly
emphasizes the necessity of making a wholehearted decision because it is not merely a matter of appearing foolish
in the sight of others (14:30), but a matter in which thousands of lives hang in the balance (14:31). Having spoken
of the conditions of discipleship in terms of being ready to
leave family members and of regarding one's life as already
finished, Jesus has made it clear that he is indeed asking
his followers to be ready to give up everything for his sake
(14:33). Jesus' remarks about the uselessness of salt without flavor make the same point as the parables: half-
hearted discipleship is useless. (The people of Israel placed
salt in a small cloth sack, then inserted this in the cooking
vessel for seasoning. After so many uses the salt lost its
saltiness, the sack was opened and the contents thrown
away.) The salt with savor stands for the disciple who is
ready to risk all, even life itself, in order to follow Jesus to
Jerusalem for the sake of the kingdom of God. But if one

undertakes the journey of discipleship and then leaves the path, there is disaster. To be thrown away symbolizes the negative judgment:

> *Get away from me, all you wicked people! How you will cry and gnash your teeth, when you see Abraham, Isaac, and Jacob, and all the prophets in the Kingdom of God, while you are thrown out! (13:27–28).*

Week Six

Dante referred to Luke as the scribe of the loving kindness of Jesus. The readings of this sixth week begin with Luke's faithful recounting of Jesus' loving concern for sinners and outcasts (15:1–3, 7 and 10) and concludes with Jesus' declaration that salvation has come to the house of Zacchaeus. Jesus' words to the repentant tax collector well express his mission: "The Son of Man came to seek and to save the lost" (19:10).

In sharp contrast to Jesus' tender concern for the sinners and nobodies of his day is his severe stance toward those who allow their wealth to blind them to the needs of the poor (16:19–31).

DAILY STUDY ASSIGNMENTS: WEEK SIX

Day	Luke	Commentary
1	15:1–32	pp. 164–169
2	16:1–31	pp. 169–179
3	17:1—18:8	pp. 179–187
4	18:9–30	pp. 187–191
5	18:31—19:10	pp. 192–196

6 Review Luke 15:1—19:10 in light of the reflection questions that follow.

7 Group meets for study and prayer.

1. What is the basic connection between Luke 15:1–2 and the parable of the two brothers and their loving father (also known as the parable of the prodigal son) in 15:11–32?

2. What is the point of the parable of the dishonest but astute steward in 16:1–8a? It may be noted that this parable is a "crisis parable," that is, Jesus was stressing the urgency in making a decision for conversion, for accepting his message regarding the coming or the nearness of the kingdom of God.

3. The delay of Jesus' hoped-for return was a problem for the persecuted churches in Luke's audience (17:22–37). How do the words of Jesus' parable in 18:1–8a address that problem?

4. A virtuous Pharisee, who fasts and pays tithes, goes home without being reconciled with God, but a sinful

tax collector simply asks for mercy and goes home "at rights with God" (18:14). In 19:1–10 a cheating tax collector receives salvation for making restitution and giving half his money to the poor. What Lucan themes tie these episodes together?

5. A young ruler sadly refuses to accept Jesus' invitation to discipleship "because he was very rich" (18:23). What are some of the obstacles that may prevent a twentieth century person from following Jesus? What is it in your life that may stand in the way of a more complete following of Jesus as his disciple?

The Lost Sheep, the Lost Coin, and the Two Lost Sons, 15:1–32

OVERVIEW. In Luke 5:36–38 the illustration of the old wineskins being unable to contain the new wine implied that the activity of Jesus' ministry could not be accommodated to the outlook of the traditional Jewish religious establishment. In this chapter Jesus declares that God cares about the lost ones, the sinners, and the nobodies (15:1–32). In Jesus God's long-awaited kingdom has come, and this is indeed the good news for the poor, the enslaved and all manner of sinners (see 4:18–19).

COMMENTARY. In the previous chapter Jesus was dining "at the home of one of the leading Pharisees" (14:1). Jesus had spoken of inviting the poor and the lame to supper and eating with them. Now Jesus practices what he preached as he himself "welcomes outcasts and even eats with them!" (15:2). The context that Luke provides for the three parables Jesus is about to tell is crucial: Jesus is encircled by outcasts and tax collectors who have come to hear him speak. Nearby, however, is a group of Pharisees and teachers of the law who are indignant because Jesus is eating with sinners. It is this table fellowship of Jesus with sinners that clarifies the understanding of his parables. God's search for sinners is the theme of the first two parables (15:4–10). The theme of the third parable is God's readiness to forgive. All three parables express the theme of God's rejoicing over the conversion of the sinner.

In the Semitic culture a person's identity and social status was revealed through those with whom he broke bread. Thus, the action of Jesus in eating with the outcasts of his society demonstrated his inner attitude of acceptance of those whom the religious leaders rejected as sinful. As a result, the scribes and Pharisees, representatives of another social stratum, resented Jesus' association with the outcasts. The opinion of these religious leaders was that Jesus should avoid the sinners and spend his time exclusively with the ones who kept God's law.

Knowing that these bystanders are critical of his behavior, Jesus invites the Pharisees to join in his concern for the sinner by telling the parable of the shepherd with a hundred sheep: " 'Suppose *one of you* . . . ' " (15:4). This particular shepherd spends great effort to recover one sheep, and, finding that sheep, joyfully calls friends together to celebrate. The point is clear: if a person does this over a recovered sheep, then how much more God rejoices over one repentant sinner (15:7). The ninety-nine respectable are not rendered insignificant because Jesus seeks out and eats with sinners. The one sheep was the object of the shepherd's special concern because it was in danger. The sinner is of particular concern to God because of the danger that threatens his or her salvation.

The second parable, the search for a lost coin, has the same point as the first. It is noteworthy that in this case God is likened to a woman (15:8–10).

REFLECTION. Not only is Luke the faithful recorder of Jesus' compassion, he is also the recorder of Jesus' balanced attitude toward persons of both sexes. Women are in the company of Jesus as he journeys through Israel (8:1–3). A male figure, the Good Samaritan, models the person who loves his neighbor (10:30–35), and Mary, sister of Martha, models the person who loves God (10:38–42). In this section of the Gospel account God is at one time likened to a man who rejoices over finding his lost sheep and at another likened to a woman who seeks and then joyfully finds what she has lost.

The climax of Jesus' response to his critics occurs in the third parable (15:11–32). It is joined with the two preceding stories by theme and by the refrains of "lost," "found" and "celebrate." The key figure is the father of the two sons. Neither of his boys appreciates him as a loving father. The younger son asks for his share of the inheritance, takes it and leaves. The older son takes his share of the inheritance as well (15:12). According to Deuteronomy 21:15–17, a father could divide his property before he died, with a double share of his possessions going to his first-born son. However, the father was to retain use of the property and what it produced until he died. This is what the father means when he later tells his elder son, ". . . everything I have is yours" (15:31). The younger son seems to have sold his third of the inheritance, taking the proceeds with him into a distant place where he squandered his money in reckless living. The journey to the far-away country expresses the distance that he has placed between himself and his father. Since sin can be described as separation from God, the younger son becomes a symbol of the sinner, thus connecting us with the originating cause of this story, namely, Jesus' reply to the Pharisees who had criticized him for eating with sinners (15:2). The younger son, without funds or friends, finds work feeding pigs, the most degrading kind of job a Jewish person could find. Dirty work to begin with, contact with swine also makes him religiously unclean. Starving to death, he realizes that the hired laborers on his father's farm fare better than he. Knowing that he has lived in contempt of the covenant, he realizes that he has sinned against God. Knowing that he has betrayed his father by his insulting request for his share of the inheritance and then selling it (in effect stating that he did not care if his father lived or died), he has sinned against his father (15:18). Because he did everything possible to deny the relationship between himself and his father, he intends to recognize this in his confession: "Father, I have sinned against God and against you. I am no longer fit to be called your son" (15:19). It is at the very moment that he pays heed to his sin that he finds the potential to become whole, to be healed. Filled with honest self-knowledge, he is in a position to ask forgiveness: "So he got up and started back to his father" (15:20). As the young man's father ran to meet and welcome his son, having been watching and waiting for just this moment, so God is ready to pardon and welcome the returning sinner. That is the point of the story—to express God's attitude toward sinners. Thus Jesus explains his table fellowship with the outcasts. Beneath the surface Jesus is asserting that he is acting as God's representative in his ministry to sinners. Because God loves sinners, because God seeks out the stray, because God searches for the lost ones, and because God waits with a heart filled with pity, Jesus does the same. He goes to the bars and the hangouts because those who frequent these places are the lost children of their heavenly Father.

At the very moment the wayward son is acknowledging that he no longer deserves to be his father's son (15:21), the father is ordering his hired hands to bring the robe, ring and shoes that acknowledge the boy's sonship (servants went barefooted while family members wore shoes). The fatted calf is killed to celebrate the dead son's return to life (15:24). The finding of the lost son is indeed a joyful occasion!

But the elder brother's response is one of anger and subsequent refusal to participate in the festivities. Just as the father went out to meet the younger son (15:20), so the father goes out into the field to invite the elder son to participate in the celebration (15:28). The elder son, in speaking of his working "like a slave" for his father and in describing himself as one who never disobeyed "orders," reveals that he, like his brother, considered himself in the category of "hired hand." Even though the elder son never left the property, he lacked a filial relationship with his father. Furthermore, the elder son refuses to acknowledge his brother as a brother. The elder son's expression, "this son of yours," represents how distant he is from any brotherly relationship. When the father responds, he points to the relationship he has always had with his elder son: "My son . . . you are always here with me" (15:31). Then the father tries to restore the proper perspective regarding the relationship between his two sons: "But *we* had to celebrate . . . because *your brother* was dead, but now he is alive . . ." (15:32).

Jesus told this parable to correct two mistaken notions about the way God relates to his children. Sinners are not to think of themselves as if they are rejected by God, nor are they to think of themselves as remotely related to God as a hired hand or slave is related to employer or owner. They are always the children of their Father! He is a Father who supplies robe and ring with family insignia because he never ceases caring for his children. The second notion Jesus tries to correct deals with the attitude of the Pharisees. In their excessive zeal for obeying the law, they seem to relate to God only out of a sense of obligation. The Pharisees are like hired hands trying to carry out the orders of their master.

By telling this parable Jesus is inviting the Pharisees to see themselves symbolized by the elder son. Thus the parable has brought us full circle, for the original starting point was the Pharisees' criticism of Jesus' eating with sinners (15:1–2). These sinners, Jesus tells the Pharisees, are your brothers and God loves you both. Thus Jesus implicitly invites the Pharisees to join him in eating with sinners: "But we had to celebrate and be happy because your brother was dead . . . he was lost, but now he has been found" (15:32). It is an open-ended invitation. It is very possible that in the original telling of this parable Jesus had hoped that many of the Pharisees still might accept him and his teaching about God's all-embracing love. The Father is the one who is never dead and never lost; he is always living, always found and always there.

It is likely that Luke wanted this parable to apply also to the Christians in the various churches. The story contains attitudes that both sinful and virtuous Christians could take to heart. Perhaps those members of Luke's audience who wanted difficult re-entrance requirements for lapsed or sinful Christians were in particular need of being confronted by Jesus' parables concerning our ever-merciful Father.

The Shrewd Manager, 16:1–8

Luke has provided three parables of Jesus that proclaimed God's love for sinners (15:4–32). These parables plus their setting (15:1–3) speak of the proper attitude believers should have regarding the outcast and the sinner. Now Luke addresses the issue of the faithful use of the disciple's worldly possessions. Although Luke mentions that Jesus addresses his disciples (16:1), there is no indication that the setting has changed from that stated in 15:1–2.

To see the point of the parable as Jesus originally told it, we must see its connection with Jesus' calling people to make a commitment to the kingdom of God. The story of the shrewd steward is about a person who made a decision that had an impact on the way he would live for the rest of his life.

As the parable unfolds, a servant is about to be dismissed for wasting his employer's money; he was neglecting his responsibilities (16:1). The servant's future looks very bleak. Beggary awaits him because he lacks the strength for manual labor (16:3). As he ponders the bind he is in, he receives a flash of insight and realizes how he can solve his dilemma. He then makes a decision that has a bearing on his entire future. About to lose his job, he decides to give up something in the present in view of obtaining a greater good in the future—the security of being welcomed into the homes of his master's former creditors (16:4). Calling in his master's creditors, he reduces their indebtedness by giving up his rightful commission (16:5-7). As a steward he had a right to a percentage of what he collected for his employer. In 16:8a the employer praises the steward, not for his earlier neglect of duty, but for having the foresight to give up his commission for the sake of what would be needed later on when he had no job. It is likely that this first half of verse 16:8 was the original ending of the parable.

Verse 8b seems to have been added later as a moral. The original ending praised the steward for his worldly shrewdness. The moral laments the fact that the disciples are not equally astute. The clever manager was concerned above all else with his security in this world. Jesus invites his audience to be equally concerned about their eternal future and equally clever in providing for their eternal security. Jesus was asking his audience to put themselves in the place of the steward about to lose his employment. They must make a decision as to whether they will continue to live their lives as they have been up to that point, or will they recognize the crucial importance of responding to the kingdom and reorient their lives to make the kingdom their priority? Drastic measures are needed to make their future secure.

Sayings of Jesus Related to the Right Usage of Wealth, 16:9–13

Verses 9–13 provide further applications of the theme of the parable of the shrewd manager. Luke has gathered together some of Jesus' sayings on the right usage of wealth. The admonition to befriend worldly wealth so that its diminishment will insure one's welcome into eternity (16:9) is similar to the counsel given earlier: "Provide for yourselves purses that don't wear out, and save your riches in heaven . . ." (13:33). Money spent aiding others is the best use of one's surplus goods. This usage stands in sharp contrast to those who store up the goods of this life solely for themselves, as exemplified by the man who tore down his barns in order to build larger ones (13:16–20). The parable of the rich barn-builder concludes with a warning very similar to that in verse 9: "This is how it is with those who pile up riches for themselves but are not rich in God's sight" (12:21).

Throughout his account Luke records Jesus' speaking of money as the lesser of two kinds of riches. In 16:10–11, for example, the person who can trustfully handle little things (earthly money) can be entrusted with great things ("true wealth," heavenly riches, salvation). Great care must be taken to have the right priorities (God and his great riches must come first), because one cannot equally serve both God and money (16:13).

Other Sayings of Jesus, 16:14–18

While some lawyers and Pharisees may have been avaricious men, a description of all Pharisees as those who "loved money" (16:15) would be exaggerated. In the time of Jesus the Pharisees were men devoted to studying the Hebrew Scriptures so that God's word could be applied to every aspect of daily life. Being scholars, the Pharisees did not receive or expect large incomes. Perhaps Luke intends that some of the Christian leaders recognize themselves in this portrayal of the Pharisees as persons who scoff at the teaching of Jesus regarding the right use of money. Thus the teaching of Jesus and the response of the Pharisees can lead Christians to examine their consciences with regard to their own attitudes about acquiring wealth.

Verses 16 through 18 are linked together by the idea that the Mosaic law, as interpreted by Jesus, is still valid. Verse 16 indicates that there was an age in which God led his people through the law and the prophets, an age which endured until John the Baptist. With the preaching of the good news by Jesus a new age has begun. It is difficult to interpret the words about everyone forcing a way into the kingdom. Perhaps it could be said that the believer has to force a way through the things that block one's way into the kingdom, for example, attachment to wealth (16:13), fear of those who can kill the body but not the soul (12:4), and the worries and pleasures of this life (8:14). There is struggle involved in deciding to follow Jesus into the new age as the kingdom of God is proclaimed. However, even in the new age the law continues to be valid (16:17). The age of Moses and the prophets may have ended with John, but not the intention of God that stands behind the prophetic activity that first gave the law and then upheld it (16:17).

In the teaching on divorce (16:18) Jesus seems at first glance to do away with the Mosaic law. However, his teaching is better understood as an example of the new age that is dawning with the preaching of Jesus (16:16). The law allowed a husband to divorce his wife on condition that he followed the written forms prescribed by Deuteronomy 24:1–3. In the new age, Jesus teaches, divorce and remarriage are adultery.

In order to understand this "change" in the law, it is helpful to examine Jesus' teaching on divorce and remarriage in Matthew 19:3–9. Some Pharisees had come to Jesus and attempted to trap him by getting him to take sides in a contemporary rabbinic dispute about Deuteronomy 24:1–3: "Does our Law allow a man to divorce his wife for whatever reason he wishes?" (Mt 19:3). The Pharisees were asking Jesus to side either with the strict interpreters (who allowed divorce only in the case of adultery) or with the liberal interpreters (who allowed a man to divorce his wife for a number of trivial reasons, even the burning of a meal).

Refusing to side with either one of these schools of thought, Jesus cited Genesis 1:27 and 2:24 as the authentic expression of God's intention for man and woman:

> *Haven't you read the scripture that says that in the beginning the Creator made people male and female? And God said, "For this reason a man will leave his father and mother and unite with his wife, and the two will become one" (Mt. 19:4–5).*

The Pharisees respond by citing the words of Moses regarding the written notice of divorce (Dt 24:1ff; Mt 19:7). Jesus answers them by stating that Moses merely permitted divorce because the people were so hard to teach (literally, their hard-heartedness). Jesus then reasserts what

God had intended from the beginning (Gen 2:24) and concludes that divorce and remarriage do not conform to the will of the Father (Mt 19:9). The teaching of Jesus in Luke 16:18 does not do away with the Mosaic law (16:17) but makes it even more demanding. Because of the new power of God at work in the ministry of Jesus, older concessions to human hard-heartedness are obsolete. Jesus asks his disciples to live according to the original will of God.

REFLECTION. In light of the fact that Catholics are struggling with the issue of divorce and remarriage and in light of the fact that the teaching of Jesus is of lasting significance for all of his disciples, deep and prayerful consideration is necessary. The permanent commitment of husband and wife to each other in marriage is noble and sacramental, reflecting the permanent love of Jesus for the Church (see Eph 5:31–32). And yet marriages fail. The ideal expressed by Jesus is often unrealized. In the Eastern Orthodox Church divorce and remarriage have always been reluctantly accepted, but in the Western (Roman Catholic) Church the teaching of Jesus on permanent marriage has long ago been turned into law. The teaching of Jesus in 16:18 is important, but so are his other teachings. Church teaching has not treated Jesus' teachings on turning the other cheek, selling all one's possessions, lending yet expecting nothing back, etc., as absolutely binding. Recognizing this, members of the Church are asking this question: Without denying the teaching of our Lord, can the Church recognize that in fact marriages can fail? The question can be answered with a yes. Catholics may divorce and still remain full participating members of the Church.

What about the divorced person who wants to marry

again or who has already remarried? Regarding these delicate situations, Pope John Paul II has pointed out that two equally important principles apply: " . . . that of compassion and mercy, whereby the Church . . . ever seeks to offer . . . the path of return to God and of reconciliation with him. The other principle is that of truth and consistency . . . " (*Apostolic Exhortation on Reconciliation and Penance,* #34). According to Church teaching, a person who has been validly married may not remarry. However, every Catholic has the right to ask, through a priest, the diocesan marriage tribunal to investigate the marriage to see if it was sacramentally valid. The tribunal may grant an annulment, a declaration that the marriage in question lacked a necessary requirement. The persons are then free to marry in the Church.

More and more the Church is reaching out to separated and divorced Catholics. Not so very long ago divorced Catholics were not very welcome in a parish community. A separated Catholic was a threat; a divorced Catholic was expendable. Leaders in the Church, fearing that compassion for the divorced might lessen the esteem for permanent marriage, had lost sight of the way Jesus ministered to the hurting people of his day. In the 1970s attitudes began to change. The North American Conference of Separated and Divorced Catholics (NACSDC) was founded and now has a network of over one thousand chapters in which separated, divorced and widowed persons support and minister to one another. Clergy and laity, married and single, men and women in vows, the separated and the divorced began to realize what Karl Rahner had pointed out: "The person is the ultimate sacrament of God's love." Together these people from different life-situations, by their acceptance of each other, by their readiness to share the hurt and the hope, by their compassion for one another, became sacraments, that is, signs of God's love for one another.

As a result the majority of dioceses in the United States are today ministering to those whose marriages have painfully ended in divorce. In parishes everywhere support groups are being established, often through the aid of diocesan Family Life Offices. Confessors, spiritual directors, deacons, and persons in many other ministries stand ready to aid those who are in deep need of compassion, advice and understanding. Beginning Experience weekends for the widowed and the divorced are available throughout the United States to help people sort out their lives in relation to God, to others and to themselves as they move beyond the past into a tomorrow with less grief and greater hope.

Married couples would do well to reflect on their commitment to each other in light of the key teachings of Jesus in this Gospel account—in terms of forgiveness, prayer, perseverance in adverse circumstances, fidelity, striving to love, and following the lead of the Spirit. We can view ourselves and our spouses in the light of Jesus' teaching that all persons are loved by God, be they poor or rich, failures or successes, sinners or the pious. The entire Gospel could be seen as urging married persons to love one another with patience and tenderness, to strive to keep open the lines of communication, to seek ways of resolving the inevitable conflicts, to be kind and compassionate, to be willing to forgive, to listen to each other, to begin again and again, to appreciate the mystery of the other, and to make a continuing personal commitment to their marriage relationship.

The Rich Man and Lazarus, 16:19–31

COMMENTARY. Jesus continues to address the Pharisees who had ridiculed his teaching because they were "lovers of money" (16:14–15). The parable of the rich man and Lazarus, his neighbor (see 10:36–37), has two key points. First, the situations of the rich and the poor will be reversed in the world to come. Second, if the rich will not heed the law and the teachings of the prophets, nothing, not even a messenger risen from the dead, will lead them to repenance. The shrewd steward who made a decisive gesture to insure his future was a model for Jesus' hearers to imitate (16:1–8). In this parable, the rich man models the kind of behavior that is self-destructive. Such behavior is to be given up no matter what would be the cost of conversion.

To begin with, Jesus sketches a picture of a man living every day "in great luxury" while another man, Lazarus, lives in circumstances exactly the opposite. Whereas the rich man dresses in the finest clothes, Lazarus wears the sores resulting from grave malnutrition (16:20). Brought to the very door of the rich man, Lazarus hoped for some scraps of food from the rich man's table, but even this desire went unfulfilled (16:21). Then he died. He died without receiving a single act of kindness (see 10:37), because the rich man completely ignored him. Then the rich man died. He ended up in hell not because he was rich but because he was deliberately deaf and blind to the needs of his neighbor. He was judged on his utter indifference to the plight of the poor. Even in the place of punishment he remains unrepentant. His attitude toward Lazarus shows that he regards Lazarus as someone who is to serve his needs—the rich man wants Lazarus to be sent to hell to bring him relief (16:24).

Abraham responds by first reminding the rich man of

the way circumstances are reversed when one enters eternity; then Abraham points out the gulf between the rich man and Lazarus. It is as if Abraham were saying, "All those years when you were living in great luxury a greater and greater distance grew up between Lazarus and you. Now he has died and has come here to be with me, and you have to stay the same distance away from him as you were when you both lived. Now it is too late to do anything to change where you are."

Then the rich man had another need. He still thinks of Lazarus in terms of utility, in this case as a messenger to warn his five brothers (16:27–28). Abraham informs the rich man that Moses (the law) and the prophets are warning his brothers. But the rich man argues that the law and the prophets are insufficient; his brothers need Lazarus risen from the dead to convince them to turn from their sins (16:30). Abraham replies that not even miracles can save those who are determined to live without mercy for others. The rich man's request is turned down because it would accomplish nothing. The believing community may see in verse 30 a reference to the resurrection of Jesus. If people are not disposed to seeing the Scriptures being fulfilled in Jesus, they would not be inclined to believe even though Jesus has risen from the dead.

REFLECTION. The rich man and his five brothers had their warning in Moses and the prophets. Apropos to the parable is this excerpt from Deuteronomy:

> If in any of the towns in the land that the Lord your God is giving you there is a fellow Israelite in need, then do not be selfish and refuse to help him. . . . Give to him freely and unselfishly, and the Lord will bless you in everything you do. There will always be some Israelites who are poor and in need, and so I command you to be generous to them (Dt 15:7–11).

We can imagine Abraham replying to the rich man: "It's much more than the issue of Lazarus visiting your brothers. The problem is they don't want to hear. They don't want to see. Remember when you were living? You didn't want to see starving Lazarus. You ignored him because you wanted the best things to eat and wear. Your brothers are no different. They don't want to see either, because if they did, it would cost them something."

When Pope John Paul II came to the United States in 1978, he celebrated the Eucharist with 80,000 people in Yankee Stadium. In his homily he spoke about the parable of the rich man and Lazarus: "We cannot stand idly by when thousands of human beings are dying of hunger. . . . We cannot stand idly by, enjoying our own riches and freedom, if, in any place, the Lazarus of the twentieth century stands at our doors." The question being asked of us is: Can we discern the Lazarus of the twentieth century? Our salvation may be at stake.

Sin, Brotherly Correction, Faith, 17:1–6

COMMENTARY. As Luke has given the setting, Jesus directs his teaching sometimes to his disciples, sometimes to the Pharisees. In this section Jesus is again speaking to his disciples (17:1). Although sin is inevitable, Jesus warns his followers not to scandalize others, that is, become an obstacle to others by giving the kind of bad example that causes them to lose faith. To demonstrate how serious such scandal is, Jesus states that if one had the choice between causing someone to sin and dying a dreadful death, the better choice would be dying the dreadful death. The terrible death envisioned is that of being drowned in the sea (17:2). For the Jews the sea symbolized chaos, destruction and the fearful unknown. Those who heard Jesus realized the evil of leading others into sin.

However, when a person did sin, the disciple should correct that person. If correction is heeded, then forgiveness is to be given for as many times as the person is repentant (17:3–4). The Church that Jesus brings into being is intended to be a caring community, a loving fellowship of persons who care about each other in both their physical and their spiritual needs.

When the disciples (who include the contemporary Christians in Luke's audience) hear Jesus' teaching regarding the attitude of open-ended forgiveness, they ask for an increase of faith (17:5). The implication of their request is clear: forgiving those who wrong them is an enormous responsibility. Jesus' response lets them know that even the smallest degree of faith (comparable in size with the tiny mustard seed) is sufficient to enable his followers to keep his teaching (17:6).

The Servant-Slave's Duty, 17:7–10

This parable may have been originally directed toward the Pharisees. In the present setting the parable addresses both the Pharisees as well as the followers of Jesus. One appreciates the meaning of this parable more fully when the spirituality of the Pharisees and the situation of the servant or slave are understood.

Regarding the spiritual outlook of the Pharisees, it seems that many of them believed that those who knew the law and kept it completely were assuring themselves of salvation. The self-righteousness of the elder brother (15:29–30) can be seen as symbolizing those who expected a reward for their being faithful to the law. Perhaps the underlying assumption to this spirituality was the belief that God was just and that therefore God was obliged to grant salvation to those who kept his law to the full.

Jesus seems to have realized that this approach to salvation gave the learned an advantage over the ordinary people who were not in a position to know the law and the traditions fully, much less adhere to them to the letter. Thus Jesus critiqued the kind of relationship with God that was based on an I'll-do-this-if-you-do-that type of attitude. To make his point, Jesus spoke of the relationship between the slave and his master (17:7–9) and offered this as a model for understanding the real relationship between the believer and God.

Because the slave is a slave, he is not entitled to any reward for his service. It is his state in life to serve his master. Thus the law-keeping believer is not entitled to any reward from God. Salvation cannot be earned. Because the law expressed God's will, it was to be obeyed regardless. After a day's work in the field, the master does not say, "Come, eat the meal you have earned" (17:7–8). On the contrary, the servant has the further responsibility of preparing supper for the master. In a similar way the believer's attitude was to be one of loving readiness to serve God regardless of everything. The believer serves God because he is a believer and God is God. It is a matter of the Lordship of God; we do not serve him on condition that we get rewarded with salvation. Our authentic existence as human beings and as disciples depends on serving God unconditionally.

Jesus Heals Ten Lepers, 17:11–19

Again Luke reminds his audience that Jesus is continuing his journey to Jerusalem (17:11), the goal he had chosen with decisive resolve in 9:51. On his way, Jesus is hailed by ten lepers who plead for his mercy. Jesus directs them to follow the prescription of the law (Lv 14:2ff) which calls for their being examined by a priest who would declare them cured. Since the ten set out before they were cured, they were all expressing some faith in Jesus. However, even though all ten were cured on the way to the priest, only one returns to praise God and thank Jesus (17:15–16). That one person was a Samaritan. There is a connection between this miracle and the parable of the servant's responsibility in 17:7–10. The servant did not earn or deserve thanks from his master; he was doing his expected duty. The master is God and the servant represents the Jews who are called to obey his law. In the parable of the ten lepers, the lepers are cured by the power of God working through Jesus. God is the one who deserves thanks, but only the Samaritan comes back to praise God.

Jesus asks two questions. First, he asks: Where are the other nine? (17:17). Second, he asks: "Why is this foreigner the only one who came back to give thanks to God?" (17:18). To give thanks to God literally means to glorify God by telling of God's life-giving activity on behalf of self and others (see 17:15). The unexpected had happened: the "foreigner" manifested his grateful response for what God has done while the ones who are supposed to be God's chosen people failed to do so. Jesus declares to the Samaritan that "your faith has made you well" (17:19). The Samaritan's cure was total, that is, he was healed in body and in spirit. Of the ten who experienced the miracle of being made clean, only one experiences salvation through faith in Jesus. It is possible that this scene is intended to foreshadow the success of the Jewish-Christian missionaries in Samaria after the death of Jesus.

The Coming of the Kingdom, 17:20–37

OVERVIEW. The material in this section involves three historical periods: (1) the teaching of Jesus during his ministry; (2) the period in which the apostolic witnesses orally proclaimed what Jesus taught; (3) Luke's present application of the tradition of Jesus' teaching to the situation of the local churches in his audience. The third period, Luke's structuring of the material he has received for the benefit of the local churches, is manifest in the way he distinguishes between Jesus' teaching on the coming of the Son of Man (17:22–37) and Jesus' prophesying the fall of Jerusalem which Luke will treat later in 19:41–44 and 21:20–24. Both Mark and Matthew link the teaching on the coming of the Son of Man with the destruction of Jerusalem (Mk 13:1–27; Mt 24:1–31). Luke may have separated the words of Jesus about the coming of the Son of Man from his teaching on the destruction of Jerusalem to discourage people from thinking that the event of Jerusalem's destruction (70 A.D.) was a sign that Jesus' second coming was very close. Luke realized that the Church is called to live its faith in this world. It was clear to him that an indefinite period of history stretches out before both the Church and the world.

COMMENTARY. Once again some Pharisees question Jesus. This time they want to know when the kingdom of God would come, that is, they want to know what are the specific signs that will manifest its imminent arrival (17:20). Jesus tells them there will be no external signs. No one will be able to say, "Look, here it is!" because if someone were to say this, he or she would be wrong. Jesus declares that nothing can be observed because the kingdom is already present (17:21). The kingdom's being "within you" is not easy to interpret. In all other instances of Jesus' proclaiming the coming of the kingdom, it is not a case of the kingdom entering the person, but a case of the person accepting the invitation to enter the kingdom. This fact may be the key to understanding verse 21. It could be said that the kingdom is "within" in terms of a person's being able to decide for the kingdom and then grasp it, that is, make it part of one's framework for living in accordance with the will of God. Those who hear the word of God and live it out (6:47; 8:21; 11:26) are not only entering the kingdom, but also allowing the Kingdom or reign of God to enter them.

In verse 22 Jesus addresses his disciples, warning them against future disappointment. The phrase, "days of the Son of Man," is crucial for the understanding of this section. The title refers to the mysterious personage that appears in Daniel 7:13–14. Here a figure "like a son of man" receives the right to act as heavenly ruler and judge from God. In the Lukan context the title, "Son of Man," refers to Jesus' future vindication, his coming in triumph.

Those associated with Jesus, including the persecuted Christians in the churches for whom Luke is writing, would be expected to yearn for the days following Jesus' glorious coming (17:22). But it is a hope not likely to be experienced in the immediate future. Jesus tells his disciples, both those who are traveling to Jerusalem with him and those who are living in the 80s, to pay no heed to those who would mislead the community by declaring that Jesus had already come back (17:23). When that time comes, his appearance will be as unmistakable as lightning (17:24).

Jesus warns his followers to be prepared always, for the days of the Son of Man may come at any time. In the days of Noah the people were going about doing the ordinary things connected with human living. Then the flood hit them and all normal life was swept away. Noah was saved because, having listened to God, he was ready. Sudden judgment came to Sodom as well, but Lot escaped through his readiness. The point for the disciples: be prepared for the unexpected day on which the Son of Man will be revealed (17:30).

A shift in thought takes place in verse 31. The images portray the necessity of immediate flight to save oneself from disaster. One is advised to leave all possessions behind because a moment of hesitation would involve catastrophe. Hence, if a person is on the flat roof of his home when the time comes, he must not take the time to re-enter the home (an exterior staircase led from roof to ground) to take any belongings. Lot's wife was indecisive; by turning around to look back she lost all. The disciple's willingness to lose life (seen in 9:24) is the basic principle underlying the examples Jesus speaks about. Attachment to one's possessions (17:31) and attachment to one's life (17:33) bring disaster to the disciple who has pledged to follow Jesus at all costs (see 9:57–62).

The thought in verses 34–36 follows the point made in the reference to Noah. He was ready while the others, engaged in eating, drinking and marrying, were not. In the case of the two sleeping persons, the two women at the mill and the two men in the field, they were seemingly the same. However, in the context of this discourse, their inner attitudes greatly differ. On the basis of their inner preparedness, one escapes the judgment, the other does not. The separation process is symbolic of judgment. The coming of Jesus will involve everyone. Those who prepared for his coming by striving to be faithful to Jesus' teaching will be received into the kingdom; those who are not prepared will be left behind.

The question "Where, Lord?" asked by the disciples

(17:37) may refer to the place where people will be taken or left (17:34). Jesus' answer is enigmatic. Jesus' reply may mean that there will be no explicit signs regarding the time of judgment, but that judgment will come as surely as vultures will find the carcass of a dead animal (17:37).

The Parable of the Widow and the Judge, 18:1–8

Jesus' instruction on the final coming of the Son of Man is brought to a conclusion with a parable on the need for continual prayer. Luke interprets the parable in his introduction: "Jesus told his disciples a parable to teach them that they should always pray and never become discouraged" (18:1). The situation Jesus describes is bleak. No one would expect a favorable outcome for a powerless widow whose hopes rest upon a corrupt judge who respects neither God nor society (18:3–4). However, her persistence, similar to that of the man who kept on asking his neighbor for bread to feed a guest who had come at midnight (11:5–8), wins over the judge.

If an unscrupulous judge finally provides the widow with justice, then how much more will God hear the prayers of the members of the believing community (18:7)! Apparently the first century Christians were discouraged. If there was much hope for the second coming of Jesus, a delay in his arrival would be tolerable in the ordinary circumstances of human living. However, when believers are being subjected to harassment, economic sanctions, imprisonment and even death, when apostasy is increasing and hope is decreasing, then the delay becomes almost unbearable. This parable of Jesus was especially applicable for those who needed reassurance that God would soon act on their behalf. Unlike the corrupt judge, God will quickly act on their behalf (18:8a). The decisive issue, however, is whether the communities of believers will persevere in faith until the final coming of the Son of Man (18:8b).

The Parable of the Pharisee
and the Tax Collector, 18:9–14

This parable is the last of the parables of Jesus that are found only in Luke. Like the preceding parable of the widow and the judge, also unique to Luke, this parable begins with a statement of purpose; it is addressed to those "who were sure of their own goodness and despised everybody else" (18:9). Jesus is calling all people to repentance. In this case he calls the "good" people to turn away from their pride and contempt of others. Repentance is linked with a person's recognition of his or her sinfulness. The Pharisee in the parable attributes his faithfulness in obeying the law to his own ability, rather than to God's grace. Thus he distorts the most basic relationship between himself and God (18:11–12).

While the Pharisee does perform genuine acts of piety such as fasting, tithing and keeping the commandments, he is blind to his self-righteousness and lack of compassion. His arrogance and pride prevent him from doing the one thing that is truly necessary: acknowledging his dependence on God's mercy. In sharp contrast to the Pharisee is the tax collector. He recognizes his sinfulness and seeks God's forgiveness (18:13). Because the tax collector asked God for mercy, he went home in the right with God (18:14). The Pharisee, holding other people in contempt and assuming God's role of judging others, left the temple no better off than when he had entered. As long as people repress awareness of their sinfulness and need of mercy, they cannot grow in their relationship with God.

Jesus Blesses the Children, 18:15–17

At this point Luke returns to his Markan source, which he departed from when he began to recount Jesus' journey to Jerusalem (9:51). Luke utilizes the story of Jesus and the children to demonstrate the kind of humility that the Pharisee lacked (18:11–12) and to further clarify Jesus' answer to the Pharisees who had asked about the signs regarding the coming of God's kingdom (17:20).

While Mark states that parents brought their "children" (Mk 10:13) to be blessed by Jesus, Luke writes that "babies" were presented for a blessing (18:15). In this way Luke emphasizes the state of dependence and the absence of self-sufficiency that characterize the lives of infants. Jesus then asserts that the kingdom of God "belongs to such as these" (18:16). These children stand in sharp contrast to the Pharisee who had thanked God that he, the adult believer and keeper of the whole law, was not like the sinful tax collector. Then, implicitly answering the question the Pharisees had asked about the timing of the coming of the kingdom in 17:20, Jesus declares that entry into God's kingdom depends upon the disciple's receptivity to the gift of salvation (18:17).

The Rich Man, 18:18–30

Having indicated the qualities needed for entrance into the kingdom, Luke now records an event in which Jesus speaks of wealth as an obstacle to entering the kingdom. The incident begins with a Jewish leader asking Jesus the same question asked earlier by a Pharisee: "What must I do to receive eternal life?" (10:25 and 18:18). While the Pharisee addressed Jesus as "Teacher," the Jewish leader used the title of "Good Teacher." Jesus questions the man's use of "good," perhaps referring to the opening verse of several psalms, "Give thanks to the Lord, because he is good" (Pss 106:1; 118:1; 136:1). Jesus thus points to the testimony of the Hebrew Scriptures as the basis for declaring that God alone deserves to be described as good because God is the source of all goodness.

Jesus then refers the man to the second portion of the Ten Commandments, those dealing with a person's responsibilities to one's neighbor (18:20). When the man replies that he has obeyed these commandments all his life, Jesus points out that there is one thing he lacks (18:22). That one thing is a relationship with Jesus and his disciples. The obstacle that stands in the young leader's way is his wealth. Therefore, Jesus counsels him to sell "all you have," giving the proceeds to the poor, and then "follow me" (18:22). At stake in the renunciation of his riches is total generosity toward others (give the money to the poor) and perfect freedom in following Jesus.

When we read that the leader "became very sad, because he was very rich" (18:23), we see that this is a story of self-discovery. The young man discovers that he is so attached to his wealth that he is not able to accept the invitation to follow Jesus. His life-style is really of greater value to him than eternal life. Because receiving the gift of eternal life is the same as entering the kingdom, Jesus points out the great difficulty rich people have in entering the kingdom (18:24). Discipleship is the cost of the kingdom, but for the rich this cost may be too high.

When Jesus declares that a rich person will have greater difficulty in entering the kingdom than a camel has in passing through a needle's eye, the crowd is shocked. In that culture riches had commonly been interpreted as a sign of God's approval. Their thought is similar to this: if the rich people, who are so obviously blessed by God, will have such difficulty in receiving eternal life, how is anyone going to be saved? In reply Jesus stresses the point he made when he declared that his disciples must be like children who are humbly open to receive the gift they can in no way earn: what is humanly impossible is possible for God (18:27).

The episode has led Peter to reflect on the experience of the disciples (18:28). They have left their homes to follow Jesus; will this renunciation meet the requirements for entering the kingdom? Jesus affirms their choice. They have put their trust in God; they live with an attitude of detachment, valuing the kingdom above all else. They are doing the one thing necessary (18:22). Not only will eternal life be theirs, but also abundant life on earth (18:30).

REFLECTION. The incident of Jesus calling the rich young ruler can have many applications. In the light of the growing concern for social justice and putting into practice the preferential option for the poor, what could this episode say about our contemporary situation? We recognize that there are vast differences between our twentieth century society and Luke's first century Greco-Roman civilization. Then the population was small; there was little "social consciousness" with regard to the dignity of human beings. Most people saw the lot to which they were born as a matter handed out by the impersonal whims of fate. Luke tried to raise the consciousness of his readers, so that those who were well-to-do would share their wealth by giving to the poor.

It would seem, in light of the tremendous complexities of our world's economic systems, that our almsgiving would not change things. We might find ourselves thinking, "Even if I sold everything I have, gave the money to the poor and followed Jesus, what would my personal charity really accomplish?" But to ask this question is to start at the wrong place—as if what counted was only that which would change the world. The most important aspect is the change that takes place in ourselves. The starting point for real change is the realization that following Jesus means personal conversion. Jesus was calling the rich ruler to personal conversion. Jesus' invitation to "come and follow me" is the key to the application of this passage to our lives. If we start at personal conversion, then the smallest step taken or the most insignificant contribution made is decisive.

It is self-defeating to hold that our giving accomplishes very little in the face of the great changes needed in our social structures. It is true that many of society's problems cannot be solved by merely increasing charitable contributions to the poor. But it is also true that other action can be taken. Individuals are not powerless; they can work at changing the social structures that keep people poor and oppressed. On the one hand the problems of bad housing, poverty, racial discrimination and depressed life-styles are problems that have to be worked on by those who experience them. On the other hand, the poor alone can never resolve the problems that bring misery to their lives. While our society and our government have a primary responsibility in the shaping of a just society, the poor need those who operate the soup kitchens as well as those who can help the poor organize themselves to change the systems so they serve human needs. Jesus' invitation to use one's time, talent and worldly goods to help the poor continues in our own day.

Jesus Speaks a Third Time About His Death, 18:31–34

In answering Peter's concern about his eligibility for the kingdom, Jesus affirmed Peter's commitment (18:28–30). By speaking of his approaching death, Jesus now tries to broaden the disciples' perspective: following their Master means not only being gifted in the present age and in the age to come (18:30), but also grief in the humiliation and death of Jesus (18:31–33). The journey to the kingdom is along the same way traveled by the suffering servant of God (see 4:1–13; 9:31). The journey on which Jesus embarked with resolute determination (9:51) will soon be completed in the city where the prophets have met their deaths: Jerusalem (13:33). Although this third mention of the passion is the most explicit of all (see 9:22, 45), the twelve do not comprehend what Jesus tries to tell them. Luke repeats this three times: "But the disciples did not understand any of these things; the meaning of the words was hidden from them, and they did not know what Jesus was talking about" (18:34). This statement by Luke is one of the clearest declarations that during the days of Jesus' ministry his followers were unable to grasp much of the significance of Jesus' deeds and teachings. Their eyes would only be opened fully by the risen Christ. Then, in the decades that followed the resurrection, they came to understand (see 24:31–35).

Jesus Heals a Blind Beggar, 18:35–43

Luke skips over Mark's account of the dispute about which of the disciples would be the greatest (Mk 10:35–45), but later places a shortened form of this episode in the recounting of the Last Supper (22:24–27). In Mark's account the blind man is healed by Jesus as he leaves the city of Jerico (Mk 10:46–52), but Luke locates the healing at the time Jesus enters the city. Afterward Jesus encounters Zacchaeus in the city and accepts the tax collector's hospitality (19:1–10).

This episode begins with the blind beggar's request for an explanation of the gathering of people taking place. Upon hearing that "Jesus of Nazareth is passing by," the blind man cries out, referring to the Davidic lineage of Jesus first spoken of by the angel Gabriel (1:32–33). In the man's request for mercy Jesus perceives the depth of his faith. Following the healing we find three typical Lucan notes: the formerly blind man becomes a disciple of Jesus, he gives thanks to God at work in Jesus, and finally the crowd, witnessing the healing, offers praise to the Lord.

REFLECTION. What a beautiful moment in the life of Jesus this is! Although physically blind and destitute, the man outside Jericho is alive to God's presence and work in Jesus. His faith-filled cry for mercy leads him to new fullness of life, both physical and spiritual. So often when we are beset by difficulties, we lose faith, we lose heart, we grumble that God has abandoned us. Far better to cry out, "Jesus! Son of David! Have mercy on me!" with expectant faith. Then we learn anew of Jesus' deep concern for us (18:41).

Jesus and Zacchaeus, 19:1–10

OVERVIEW. The account of Jesus' encounter with Zacchaeus may be seen as a summary of Jesus' ministry. From the time he began to preach in Galilee through his journey to Jerusalem, Jesus has ministered to all. He has a particular concern for sinners. This episode has strong ties with Jesus' eating with sinners, the public criticism of his doing so, and his reply in terms of the three parables of God's mercy (15:1–32). It is also related to the parable of the self-righteous Pharisee and the sinful tax collector who stood at the back of the temple while he humbly asked God to be merciful to him, a sinner (18:9–14). There are connections with the story of the rich young ruler who would not follow Jesus because it meant that he would have to sell his possessions and give to the poor (18:18–23). The ruler "was very rich" and his refusal to follow prompted Jesus to declare how great is the difficulty for a rich man to enter heaven (18:24–25). In the story of the conversion of Zacchaeus we see how it is possible for even a rich person to be saved: by paying attention to Jesus. That is the one thing needed (see 10:42). That will lead to making restitution for injustice and sharing one's wealth with the poor.

COMMENTARY. Zacchaeus was rich and he probably amassed his wealth by using his office as chief tax collector, which meant that he would have been in charge of a group of tax collectors operating around Jericho. There is further insight into his character and the means he employed to become wealthy in his declaration that he would make amends to those he "cheated." The expression in Greek refers to the idea of extorting money by the use of force. It is likely that he collected taxes in the company of an armed escort in order to pressure people to hand over more money than was due. This brief profile of Zacchaeus shows him to be a greedy, dishonest extortionist, collaborating with the Roman forces and making himself rich at the expense of his countrymen.

It seems that Jesus knows the man and his reputation,

for when he sees Zacchaeus in the tree, he decisively takes the initiative by inviting himself to the home of the tax collector: "Hurry down, Zacchaeus, because I must stay in your house today" (19:5). The phraseology Jesus uses, "I *must* stay," conveys the idea that God's plan is being enacted in the present moment. The same sense of urgent and decisive action Jesus has expressed on other occasions:

> "Didn't you know that I had to be in my Father's house?" (2:49)

> "I must preach the Good News about the Kingdom of God in other towns also" (4:43).

> "The Son of Man must suffer much and be rejected . . ." (9:22).

Whereas the rich ruler turned away from Jesus "filled with sadness" (18:23), Zacchaeus welcomes Jesus "with great joy" (19:6). When the people object to Jesus' going to the home of such a sinner as Zacchaeus (19:7), they are simply giving voice to the popular and common sense view that good persons should have nothing to do with those who are seemingly outside the scope of God's concern. Zacchaeus responds to the crowd's objection by declaring that he is ready to repent. As he accepts Jesus into his home, he states that he will give half of his wealth to the poor and that he will make up for his injustice by making a fourfold restitution (19:8), an amount that is far more than the law required (see Lv 6:1–5). Like the tax collector standing at the back of the temple (18:13–14), Zacchaeus faced the painful recognition of his sinfulness. Because he does so, Jesus declares that salvation has come to Zacchaeus and his family; his previous sinful way of life notwithstanding, Zacchaeus retains his membership in God's people as a son of Abraham (19:9).

By referring to himself as the Son of Man who came "to seek and save the lost" (19:10), Jesus identifies himself with the shepherd who left the ninety-nine sheep to find the one who was lost (15:5–6). Zacchaeus represents the one sinner who repents, thereby causing more joy in heaven than the ninety-nine who have no need of repentance (15:7).

REFLECTION. We might use our imaginations and ask what happened in Zacchaeus' household the day after Jesus left? Their resources are now sorely depleted by restitution; half of what was left had been given to the poor. From now on the honest collecting of taxes will not yield a large income. A radical change in life-style faces the whole family. Zacchaeus' wife will no longer be attended by servants; when she shops, she will no longer be able to afford luxuries. The sons will not have access to capital with which they could start businesses or go to the prestigious university. The daughters will not have the dowries with which to attract the best suitors. Perhaps all members of the family will be asking, "Was our salvation worth the cost?" What kind of parables could we draw between this imaginary "day after" and our own concerns for the economic security of our family? Where do we draw the line between our need for security in this life and our need for that kind of conversion that means salvation?

Week Seven

Having told a parable to dissuade his followers from any expectation that the kingdom would come at the moment he reached Jerusalem (19:11–27), Jesus enters Jerusalem and begins his teaching ministry in the temple (19:28–48). He is indeed the Messiah, but he does not conform to Israel's popular expectations.

As Jesus carries on a daily ministry of teaching in the temple, the Jewish leaders become increasingly hostile. When his enemies fail to trap him in his teachings (20:1–40), they look for a way of doing away with him (22:1–2).

Luke records Jesus' apocalyptic discourse in a way that focuses attention on the persecution of the disciples and the destruction of Jerusalem, while the events accompanying the end of the world are shifted to the indeterminate future (21:5–36).

As the opposition to Jesus increases, he takes elaborate precautions to make sure he will be able to celebrate one final Passover meal with his friends (22:3–13). During that meal Jesus links God's deliverance of Israel with his own approaching passion and death by identifying bread and wine with his body and blood to be given and shed for his disciples (22:14–20).

In the solemn setting of this last supper with his friends, Jesus warns them of hardships and temptations, while giving them final instructions for overcoming those trials. Even Peter's faith will be severely shaken, but it will not fail (22:24–38).

DAILY STUDY ASSIGNMENTS: WEEK SEVEN

Day	Luke	Commentary
1	19:11–48	pp. 200–204
2	20:1–47	pp. 204–210
3	21:1–38	pp. 210–218
4	22:1–13	pp. 218–219
5	22:14–38	pp. 219–230

6 Review Luke 19:11–22:38 in light of the reflection questions that follow.

7 Group meets for study and sharing.

1. Jesus' parable of the gold coins (19:11–27) was both remembered and reinterpreted by the early Christians. How can you reinterpret or apply this parable to yourself, your parish or your diocese?

2. Jesus wept for Jerusalem because the people living there did not recognize the time when God came to save them (see 19:41–44). What applications could you make with regard to our own civilization?

3. Do wars, earthquakes and persecution of Christians mean that the end of the world is near (21:5–38)?

4. Share with each other how Luke's recounting of the Last Supper (22:14–23) can help us to participate more completely in the celebration of the Eucharist.

5. What do Jesus' words regarding the new covenant (Lk 22:20) mean with respect to the Mosaic covenant? Why is the Mosaic covenant still valid?

6. What relationship do you think Luke may be making between Peter's declaration, "You are God's Messiah" (9:20), and Jesus' statement, "I have prayed for you, Simon, that your faith will not fail" (22:32).

The Parable of the Gold Coins, 19:11–27

COMMENTARY. Some of the disciples expect to see the arrival of the kingdom of God upon Jesus' entrance into Jerusalem. Luke indicates that Jesus told this parable to correct that mistaken expectation. When Luke's version of this parable of the gold coins is compared with Matthew's version (Mt 25:14–30), we see that Luke's recounting seems to combine two different parables. One theme deals with a king who is rejected by his countrymen (19:12, 14 and 27) and the other story deals with a man who gave his servants an amount of capital to use until he returned (19:13, 15b–26).

The parable Jesus told about the nobleman who went to become king may have been based on the deeds of Archelaus. He was the heir of Herod the Great who had gone to Rome to claim the title of king after the death of his father. A delegation of Jews had also traveled to Rome to protest his becoming king. It would have been in keeping with Archelaus' character to have taken revenge on those who did not want him as their king as indicated in 19:27. Luke seems to use the parable of the man become king as an allegory. The nobleman who goes to a far country points to Jesus who has ascended to heaven. There he becomes king. When he returns judgment will take place both for those who have received the gift of faith (the gold coins) as well as for those who refused to accept him.

The core of this parable, however, centers on the master who gives his servants a gold coin with the admonition, "See what you can earn with this while I am gone" (19:13). The master seems to be preparing his servants for receiving greater positions and gifts in the future. Thus, the servant who turns his one coin into ten receives authority over ten cities (19:16–17). Likewise, the second servant who earned five more coins receives charge of five cities (19:18–19). However, the third servant proves himself to be totally irresponsible. He is condemned and loses all (19:22–24). The point of the parable is not that he loses everything because he failed to invest his coin for an abundant yield. Rather, he loses all because he did not even take the one opportunity that was completely safe—putting it in the bank for interest (19:23)! As Jesus approaches Jerusalem he tells those who expect the kingdom of God to appear (19:11) that they must do something with their faith while they live. The warning Jesus gives is clear: those who are careless with the entrusted gift of faith are bad servants; they will be condemned by their own admitted lack of deeds (19:22). God's gracious love requires a response in action, not mere lip-service (see 6:46–49; 12:42–46).

The Triumphant Approach to Jerusalem, 19:28–40

Jesus is about to enter the city he had so resolutely set as his destination (see 9:51). At Bethany, some two miles from Jerusalem, Jesus sends his disciples ahead to find a colt not yet ridden (19:30). The request for such an animal has a messianic implication, for it indicates that the never-ridden colt has been set aside for a sacred or royal personage. The assignment is carried out according to Jesus' instructions. As Jesus nears Jerusalem, his disciples begin to praise and thank God as they recall the "great things," the signs and teachings, they have witnessed during Jesus' Galilean ministry and subsequent journey to Jerusalem. Jesus' entrance into Jerusalem on a donkey's foal recalls the words of Zechariah:

> *Rejoice, rejoice, people of Zion!*
> *Shout for joy, you people of Jerusalem!*

Look, your king is coming to you!
He comes triumphant and victorious,
but humble and riding on a donkey—
on a colt, the foal of a donkey (Zec 9:9).

The disciples' proclaiming "Peace in heaven, and glory to God" (19:38b) echoes the angels' message to the shepherds on the night of Jesus' birth: "Glory to God in the highest heaven and peace to those with whom he is pleased!" (2:14).

Verses 39 and 40 are found only in Luke. Some Pharisees in the crowd object to the loud and joyful acclamation of Jesus that comes from his disciples. Perhaps the Pharisees are friendly and fear that all this will lead to some kind of public messianic demonstration. Jesus responds prophetically. If these disciples are silenced, the inert stones would then proclaim the power of God at work in Jesus' deeds (19:40, 37).

Jesus Weeps Over Jerusalem, 19:41–44

The joyful acclamation ends suddenly, not because Jesus has heeded the request of the Pharisees, but because Jesus himself is overcome with emotion. Seeing the city of Jerusalem, Jesus weeps. The language of this section is taken from the prophetic utterances of Isaiah, Jeremiah and Hosea. Jeremiah, for example, had spoken of the destruction of Jerusalem in 587 B.C. in these terms:

The city of Zion is beautiful, but it will be destroyed; kings will camp there with their armies. . . . The Lord Almighty has ordered these kings to cut down trees and build mounds in order to besiege Jerusalem (Jer 6:2–6).

Using similar language, Jesus laments the event that could easily be foreseen in light of the tensions building up between the Jewish zealots and the Roman forces of occupation. That which "is needed for peace" (19:42) is the practice of Jesus' teaching. His arrival in the city of peace is the last chance for conversion because in Jesus God is visiting his people (19:44).

REFLECTION. Jerusalem was again destroyed by Vespasian, Titus, and the Roman armies in 70 A.D. The city did not "recognize the time" when God came to save it. Nineteen centuries later we might ask ourselves this question: What will the people of the next century say about the citizens of the United States living in the last decades of the twentieth century? In 1983 the American bishops pointed out that our nation "now possesses so many weapons as to imperil the continuation of civilization. Americans share responsibility for the current situation, and cannot evade responsibility for trying to resolve it" (*The Challenge of Peace: God's Promise and Our Response*, #326).

Our bishops, contemporary prophets, Mary of Lourdes and of Fatima plead with us—and with other great powers—to recognize what is needed for peace. Is it not tragic to realize that the weapons which threaten the very existence of our planet are stored in the armories of the largely Christian nations (Russia included) of the world? The opportunity before us now may be the realization that one does not think oneself into a new way of living, but that one lives oneself into a new way of thinking.

Jesus Goes to the Temple, 19:45–48

COMMENTARY. Luke shortens considerably Mark's account of what Jesus did when he drove the buyers and sellers from the temple's court of the Gentiles (the place where secular coins were changed into temple money and where animals for sacrifice were purchased). As justification for his action Jesus cites the words of Yahweh, "My Temple will be called a house of prayer . . ." (Is 56:7) and "Do you think that my Temple is a hiding place for robbers?" (Jer 7:11). Having directed attention to the purpose of the temple as the place to offer prayer, Jesus begins to teach there "every day" (19:47). Luke tells us that a new phase of Jesus' ministry has begun, a period of teaching in the temple, where people listened intently to his words. However, while the people hang on Jesus' every word, the chief priests, teachers of the law and the leaders desire to kill him (19:48). But first they try to tarnish his reputation in the eyes of the people by attempting to undermine his authority (20:1–8), or by trapping him in a treasonous statement (20:19–26) or by reducing his teaching to absurdity (20:27–40).

The Question About Jesus' Authority, 20:1–8

The Jewish leaders first challenge Jesus on the basis of his authority. The three groups challenging Jesus (the chief priests, the teachers of the law and the elders) constitute the Sanhedrin. They ask Jesus to name his source of authority for casting out the merchants and for teaching in the temple's precincts (20:2). According to a common form in Jewish religious debates, Jesus answers by posing his own question. When, for reasons of embarrassment or fear, the religious leaders do not want to answer his question about the source of John the Baptist's right to baptize (20:3–7), Jesus tells them, in effect, that they are not competent to recognize his authority. Therefore, he will not answer their question.

The Parable of the Tenants in the Vineyard, 20:9–18

Jesus has been challenged in public. Now he publicly warns the listening crowds to be wary of their leaders by comparing them with unscrupulous tenant farmers who will stop at nothing to take possession of another's vineyard. The parable was unmistakably aimed at the Jewish leaders—the vineyard is clearly Israel and they are the official stewards of Israel's heritage. The story is based on Isaiah 5:1–7. The concluding verse declares:

> *Israel is the vineyard of the Lord Almighty;*
> *the people of Judah are the vines he planted.*
> *He expected them to do what was good,*
> *but instead they committed murder.*
> *He expected them to do what was right,*
> *but their victims cried out for justice (Is 5:7).*

The parable Jesus tells takes the form of an allegory in which the vineyard's owner is God, the servants are prophets and the son is Jesus himself. When the time comes for the owner to receive his share of the fruits of the vineyard, he sends a servant to collect them. When this servant is beaten and sent back empty-handed, a second and a third are sent. Each is treated more shamefully than his predecessor. Finally, the owner's "own dear son" (20:13) is sent. The son is killed outside the vineyard (as Jesus was crucified outside Jerusalem), with the tenants thinking that they could thus become the owners of the property. If they presumed that the owner had died, they were mistaken. In verse 16 the owner takes action against them and then leases the vineyard to new tenants (perhaps this is a reference to the Gentiles who have entered the Church).

As the crowd expresses its dismay over the fate of the wicked tenants who represent their leaders, Jesus responds by asking what else could be the meaning of the Scripture (Ps 118:22) when it states that the stone rejected by the builders becomes the most important of all (20:17)? In a likely reference to a Jewish proverb, "Whether the pitcher falls on the stone or whether the stone falls on the pitcher—woe to the pitcher!" Jesus tells those who reject him that their own judgment is inevitable (20:18).

The Question About Paying Taxes to Caesar, 20:19–26

Jesus' parable and application are blunt and uncompromising. The chief priests and teachers of the law want to arrest Jesus then and there, but they are deterred by their fear of the people. So they plot to trap Jesus in either a treasonous statement against the Roman government or an unpopular interpretation of the law that would call upon the Jews to pay taxes to their oppressor (20:20–22). The question asked involves a poll-tax levied on the male inhabitants of Israel in 6 A.D. The tax was paid directly to Rome, using a silver denarius minted for this particular taxation.

While the question includes serious civil implications, it has an even more important theological dimension: Is it permissible to pay the tax according to the Mosaic law? Jesus does not immediately answer the question put to him by the spies. First he draws an answer from his questioners regarding the image on the coin of tribute (20:24). Then Jesus replies "Pay to the Emperor what belongs to him, and pay to God what belongs to God" (20:25). It is important to note that Jesus is not declaring that there are two separated realms of existence—God's and Caesar's. Jesus saw everything under the Lordship of God, whether it was the Israelite social order or the Roman system. He was teaching that only to the extent that Caesar's system was in accord with the will of God could Caesar expect obedience. That is why Jesus could stand in opposition to Herod, the fox who ruled by the empowerment of Rome (see 13:31–33). That is also why Jesus will warn his followers to expect opposition from Caesar's realm as they are arrested and brought before kings and governors (see 21:12–15). In sum, Jesus' answer means this: obey the emperor in matters of civil government (where the law makes no demands), for this is also obedience to God himself. But where God has spoken through the law (and particularly if there should arise a conflict between the law and the demands of the emperor), God alone is to be obeyed.

Jesus made no attempt to define whether Caesar has a right to rule or what does belong to him. Yet this is clear: a person's entire life belongs to God; obedience to the state which does not compromise this commitment is legitimate. Jesus' reply leaves the spies speechless with amazement (20:26).

REFLECTION. We cannot divide our lives into completely separate realms, as if whatever belongs to secular life is not subject to God's rule or reign. The state (the realm of Caesar) is not absolute; it too is bounded by the authority of the Creator of all. We are obligated to follow the just laws of society, but if they are unjust we are bound in conscience to work to change them. Thus the Second Vatican Council pointed out that Christians should "strive to discharge their earthly duties conscientiously and in response to the Gospel spirit." Religion does not consist "in acts of worship alone" and believers miss the mark if they imagine that "they can plunge themselves into earthly affairs in such a way as to imply that these are altogether divorced from the religious life. This split between the faith which many profess and their daily lives deserves to be counted among the more serious errors of our age" (*Pastoral Constitution on the Church in the Modern World*, art. 43).

The Question About Rising From Death, 20:27–40

This is the only instance in which Luke pays particular attention to the Sadducees. They were those Jews from whose ranks the temple priests were chosen. The Sadducees were theological conservatives, accepting only the first five books of the Hebrew Scriptures (the Torah) as inspired. They did not believe in an individual life after death that was attainable through resurrection. Their scenario about the woman who had outlived seven husbands and their question about whose wife she will be when the dead rise have the purpose of reducing belief in the resurrection to an absurdity (20:29–33).

The Messiah teaching cited by the Sadducees in verse 28 is taken from Deuteronomy 25:6. If a man died childless, the living brother had an obligation to marry the widow in order to father children on behalf of the deceased. This would continue the name and family of the one who had died, thus providing a limited kind of "survival after death." This practice arose long before belief in eternal life gained some acceptance in Judaism (about 100 B.C.).

Jesus' reply to the Sadducees is twofold. First, he points out that their understanding of the resurrection is too materialistic. The risen life will not be a mere extension of life in this world. There will be a new level of interpersonal relationships, based on the reality that all are children of God (20:35–36). Second, Jesus tells the Sadducees that they do not understand the Scriptures. Jesus then refers to the passage in Exodus that tells of Moses' encounter with God. God identifies himself as the God of Abraham, Isaac and Jacob (Ex 3:6). Since Moses lived long after these patriarchs had died, and since God is "the God of the living, not of the dead" (20:38), then Abraham, Isaac and Jacob must also be alive. In other words, Jesus argues like this: If God is alive, then those he loves must also be alive. We can say that life after death does not depend as much on the immortality of one's soul as it depends upon the personal love of God for the individual person. With the coming of Passover Jesus will exemplify this belief as he goes to his death entrusting himself totally to his Father (see 23:46).

The Question About the Messiah, 20:41–44

With Jesus winning over some of the Pharisees with his answer (20:39), his opponents cease questioning him (20:40). The stage is now set for Jesus to critique the practice and teaching of the Jewish leaders. He begins by asking a question about the Pharisees' belief that the Messiah would be David's descendant (20:41). (In 18:39 the blind beggar whom Jesus healed outside of Jericho had addressed Jesus as "Son of David.") When Jesus cites the opening verse of Psalm 110, and then asks how, if David called the Messiah "Lord," the Messiah can be David's descendant (20:42–44), there is the implied assertion that the Messiah is more than a human descendant of David. In the early Church the first verse of Psalm 110 became a favorite passage of early Christian liturgy and writing. Jesus was seen as both the human descendant or "Son of David" and the transcendent One who was also David's Lord.

Jesus Warns Against the Teachers of the Law, 20:45–47

Having indicated the weakness in the Jewish leaders' messianic expectation, Jesus turns to a critique of their way of life. Within the hearing of all, Jesus tells his disciples not to be deceived by the example of those who seem respectable and pious but who are actually seeking to exalt and benefit themselves. The reference to the Pharisees' taking advantage of widows (20:47a) probably refers to the taking of unjustified sums for legal advice or the using of their positions as appointed guardians of estates to take for themselves unwarranted remuneration for their services. A harder judgment will fall upon those who so misuse their positions of trust (20:47b).

The Widow's Offering, 21:1–4

Upon observing the kinds of offerings people were depositing in the temple treasury, Jesus contrasts the offerings of the well-to-do with the two coins given by a poor widow. While it seems that the offerings of the rich are more significant because of their greater monetary value, the truth is that these gifts are greatly surpassed by the small offering of the widow: "I tell you that this poor widow put in more than all the others . . . she, poor as she is, gave all she had to live on" (21:3–4). Outward appearances are one thing, interior realities are another. The widow's two copper coins (worth about fifty cents) symbolize her close relationship with God. She had such a degree of trusting openness to God that she was able to give "all she had to live on" (21:14).

Jesus Speaks of the End Times, 21:5–38

OVERVIEW. In this section Luke provides an account of Jesus' final public teaching. In one sense this is Jesus' farewell address to the people and to the majority of his followers. (He will share the Passover meal with the twelve.) Although Luke follows Mark's account closely, he changes the setting for this discourse. According to Mark, Jesus speaks these words to his disciples while looking down from the Mount of Olives. But Luke situates the discourse in the temple (21:5, 37). One of Luke's reasons for doing so is to stress how deeply Christianity is rooted in Jerusalem. The temple is the place where the angel Gabriel announced the birth of John the Baptist to Zechariah (1:11–15), where Jesus was presented to the Lord (2:22–24), where Simeon and Anna recognized Jesus as the expected one (2:25–38), where Jesus was found by his parents as he went about his Father's affairs (2:49), and where Jesus dramatically drove out the buyers and sellers so that he could teach the good news to all (19:45–20:1). After Jesus ascends to his Father, his disciples will return to the temple in order to joyfully praise God (24:52–53). In his second volume, the Acts of the Apostles, Luke will tell the story of the Church as it moved from the temple (Acts 2:46) and Jerusalem to the ends of the earth (Acts 1:8).

COMMENTARY. When some members of Jesus' audience speak of how they are impressed with the beauty of the temple, Jesus shares with them the realization he had as he entered Jerusalem (19:41–44). Temple and city will be destroyed (21:6).

The audience responds to Jesus' statement about the destruction of the temple with two questions. They want to know when the temple will be destroyed and they want to know what signs will immediately precede that event (21:7). Jesus does not answer their questions directly. The reply that he does give has two parts. First, Jesus warns his listeners not to be deceived by those who will make false claims in his name (21:8). This warning about being led astray by those posing as messianic messengers is similar to Jesus' admonition to ignore those who say "look here" or "look there" to find the Son of Man (17:23). By the mid 50s there were false messiahs who claimed that Jesus had secretly come back and therefore the end of the world was about to begin. They are not to be followed (21:8).

The second part of Jesus' reply deals with those wars and disasters that could be interpreted as indications that the end of all things has begun. Jesus states that his followers should not fear because these events of history and nature "do not mean that the end is near" (21:9). To appreciate Jesus' teaching on this point it is useful to explain one of the forms of Jewish expectation regarding the end of the world. When oppression was most bitter, the hope for God's intervention in history grew strong. When the oppression became even more intense, there developed an expectation that God's final intervention would be preceded by a series of terrible disasters in which the cosmos itself would disintegrate (see Jl 2:1–11). Jesus refers to this popular expectation of terrible events preceding the end (21:10–11) and puts these events in a different perspective. Jesus' teaching makes social and even cosmic upheaval secondary. More important is the persecution of the disciples and the opportunity this affords to give witness to the good news (21:12–13).

The disciples can face arrest and trial confidently, because Jesus will be with them: "Do not worry about how you will defend yourselves because I will give you such

words of wisdom that none of your enemies will be able to
. . . contradict what you say" (21:15). The life of the follower of Jesus is a life of on-going faithfulness, not merely
a series of superficial conversions brought about by each
natural or historical disaster. Thus, when the disciples are
betrayed (21:16) or hated (21:17) because of their commitment to Jesus, they should remember that they will not
lose a single hair from their heads (21:18). In view of the
fact that Christians were imprisoned, tortured and put to
death for the sake of Jesus, verse 18 appears to refer to a
"spiritual" safety. One's persecutors may be able to kill the
body but they are powerless to do anything more because
one's spirit is totally in the hands of the living God (see
12:7; 20:38). Jesus' words, "Stand firm, and you will save
yourselves" (21:19), remind us of his description of the
seeds that fell upon the good soil: "The seeds that fell in
good soil stand for those who hear the message and retain
it in a good and obedient heart, and they persist until they
bear fruit" (8:15).

Verses 20 to 24, dealing with the fall of Jerusalem during the Jewish-Roman War of 66–73 A.D., describe an
event that lay in the future from the point of view of Jesus
as he taught in the temple. However, from the point of
view of Luke, these verses describe an event that has already come to pass. In this section Jesus answers the questions he was asked about the time of the destruction of the
temple and the signs preceding this event (21:7), but he
does so in prophetic terms that also include the doom of
the city of Jerusalem (21:20). The prophecy of Jerusalem's
destruction also includes a warning to flee the city when
armies come to lay siege. (Jerusalem had been under siege
before, and the first temple built by Solomon had been destroyed by the Babylonians in 586 B.C.) As he have seen in
19:41–44, Jesus speaks of the destruction of Jerusalem in

biblical vocabulary. He did not need a special form of divine knowledge regarding the future to say what he did. As a man of religious sensitivity and intuition Jesus could counsel the inhabitants of the city to flee to the mountainous areas of Judea and warn those in the immediate area not to try to take refuge in Jerusalem when the armies came (21:21). Jesus was a Jew, and Jews interpreted the events of history in light of their faith in God. The prophets had declared that by turning away from God the people brought disaster upon themselves. In this same prophetic tradition Jesus speaks of "the Days of Punishment" and of "God's punishment" falling upon the people (21:22, 24). What Jesus states here echoes what God had said through Jeremiah:

> *You have committed all these sins, and even though I spoke with you over and over again, you refused to listen. . . . And so, what I did to Shiloh I will do to this Temple of mine, in which you trust (Jer 7:13–14).*

In 21:23b–24 Luke departs from his Markan source. The tribulation of women and children, the killing, and the survivors being taken into slavery to many nations had already happened by the time Luke wrote. Jesus' statement about the Gentiles (heathen) conveys the idea that there will be a period of time separating the destruction of Jerusalem from the moment when he will appear as the Son of Man. Thus, the destruction of Jerusalem is not to be viewed as the event signaling the beginning of the end, but is to be seen as the beginning of a period in which Gentiles will have a central place in God's plans (see Rom 11:11–32). This time is a time with limits, for it too will come to an end with the final coming of the Son of Man.

In verses 25 to 28 Jesus uses apocalyptic imagery (images of cosmic upheaval usually connected with God's final intervention in human history) to describe his final coming. As the natural order of things rages out of control, some will experience terrible fear (21:26). "Then the Son of Man will appear, coming in a cloud with great power and glory" (21:27). The title, "the son of Man," had associations with the apocalyptic literature written during the two centuries prior to the death of Jesus. In this passage the title is closely linked with the Book of Daniel:

> *One like a son of man coming,*
> *on the clouds of heaven;*
> *When he reached the Ancient One*
> *and was presented before him,*
> *He received dominion, glory and kingship;*
> *nations and peoples of every language serve him.*
> *His dominion is an everlasting dominion*
> *that shall not be taken away,*
> *his kingship shall not be destroyed (Dan 7:13–14, NAB).*

Just as Isaiah's image of the mysterious suffering servant of God (see Is 52:13–53:12) was applied to Jesus, so also is Daniel's symbolic title applied to Jesus in the context of his future coming at the end of the world (21:27). While the unbelievers fearfully witness the signs of Jesus' coming glory, the disciples are counseled to stand in hopeful expectation because these signs herald their immediate salvation (21:28).

The original context of verses 29 to 33 is not clear. The admonition to think of the fig tree and other trees when "these things" are seen happening (21:31) could refer to the coming of Jesus in glory (21:25–28) or to the events accompanying the destruction of Jerusalem (21:20–24). If the idea that "these things" will have taken place "before the people now living have all died" (21:32) is understood in a strictly literal or narrow sense, then it would refer to the people who are contemporaries of Jesus. If so, then "these things" would refer to the events related to the destruction of Jerusalem. However, the assertion that the witnessing of "these things" is the prelude to the coming of the kingdom of God (21:31) indicates that "these things" refer to the events heralding the coming of the Son of Man. The coming of the kingdom in its fullness is a future event that will be introduced by the return of Jesus in glory. Thus the phrase "the people now living" has a broad sense referring to the Jewish people or to the human family. Two realities will endure until the coming of the kingdom in its fullness: the human family (21:32) and the words of Jesus (21:33). Contrary to the many gloomy opinions regarding the "end of the world," Jesus' teaching gives us reason for hope. The image of the fig tree (21:29–30), with its leaves beginning to appear, speaks of new life. When dormant, the fig tree looks bare and dead; when its sap begins to flow, the tree bursts into life.

Verses 34–36 are unique to Luke. Using material from his own sources, Luke helps his readers apply the teaching of Jesus to their lives. Jesus exhorts his followers to avoid excessive eating and drinking as well as any preoccupation with "the worries of life." While anxiety about the end of the world is unnecessary (21:8–9, 28), the disciples of Jesus are to watch for the Day of the Lord's return (21:34–36).

With these words the public teaching of Jesus comes to a close. Luke summarizes Jesus' Jerusalem ministry by noting how he spent his days in teaching, rising early to instruct the people who were in the temple where they waited eagerly to listen to the rabbi from Galilee (21:37–38).

REFLECTION. Thinking about the final days and the coming of the Son of Man in glory can be frightening for many people. Because we live in an atomic age, because the United States and the Soviet Union have some fifty thousand nuclear warheads capable of indescribable destruction, some may not want to see the final coming of Jesus. Why has a consoling hope for the early believers become an unwanted possibility for contemporary disciples? Is it because so many have associated the event of Jesus' return with the atomic annihilation of our world?

As Luke separated the event of the destruction of the temple from the coming of the Son of Man, so the Church community today might separate the nuclear destruction of the world from the coming of Jesus in glory. On the one hand, the kind of thinking that makes a cause-effect relationship between human decisions to wage nuclear war and the coming of Jesus seems to make the false assumption that human beings can somehow determine what God will do. There would seem to be a contradiction between the message of the Gospel and the image of Jesus coming in glory upon the mushroom-shaped clouds of nuclear devastation. The untold sufferings and deaths of billions of people that would take place during and after nuclear warfare can hardly be seen as an event that would usher in the reign of God. On the other hand, God permitted the sinful decisions of some to bring about the redemption of all through the crucifixion of Jesus.

The goal of creation is the kingdom of God. It is true that God's reign has yet to be fully realized in the human community. But this means that each of us can live in hope. We can vividly expect, we can await with passionate longing the final triumph of Jesus. This means that there is a task for each of us, a role that each of us can play in our Church and in our world. The expectation of the coming of the Son of Man and the kingdom of God (see 21:31) can serve as a context for our faith, our love and our hope. To

the extent that we, the members of the believing community, can prayerfully say, "I am the Lord's servant; may it
happen to me as you have said" (1:38), to that extent the
coming of the Son of Man and the accompanying kingdom
of God is an event desired in hope. In this hope we can
keep vigil in expectation of Jesus' return because we expect
something good for our world. The flame of hope can then
blaze into mission—the mission of witnessing Jesus Christ
during the unknown length of time between his first and
his final comings. In this hope we find encouragement to
work to bring about the transformation of our world, not
its destruction. As the Second Vatican Council taught:
". . . the expectation of a new earth must not weaken but
rather stimulate our concern for cultivating this one. For
here grows the body of a new human family, a body which
even now is able to give some kind of foreshadowing of the
new age" (*Pastoral Constitution on the Church in the Modern
World*, art. 39).

The Plot Against Jesus; Judas' Betrayal, 22:1–6

Since the day Jesus began teaching in the temple the
chief priests and other leaders have been looking for a way
to kill Jesus, but his popularity with the people has prevented them from doing so (19:47–48; 22:2). In noting that
Jesus spent the day in the temple and the night on the
Mount of Olives (21:37–38), Luke has provided us with a
glimpse of how Jesus can be arrested without the knowledge of the people. As the feast of Passover approached, a
time of much activity and movement, Judas slipped away
to confer with Jesus' enemies. Luke attributes Judas' decision to betray Jesus to the inspiration of Satan and the desire of money (22:3, 5). Jesus' stress on detachment from

worldly wealth has gone unheeded: "No servant can be the slave of two masters . . . he will be loyal to one and despise the other. You cannot serve both God and money" (16:13).

As we have seen, Satan's role is to incite people to rebel against God's designs. Although the devil succeeds in leading Judas to betray Jesus (22:3), God's purposes cannot be ultimately frustrated. While Jesus does fall into the power of his enemies, the period during which "the power of darkness rules" (22:53) is only temporary. Just as Jesus resisted the suggestions to become a Messiah of earthly power and glory (4:1–13), so he will soon overcome death itself. Accordingly, the very betrayal of Jesus leads to the fulfillment of God's purposes. As the Scriptures have indicated, it was necessary that the Messiah suffer in order to enter the glory of resurrection (see 24:26, 46).

Jesus Prepares To Eat the Passover Meal, 22:7–13

Jesus sends Peter and John to prepare for the Passover (22:8–12) with instructions that have overtones of secrecy similar to the instructions given immediately before his entrance into Jerusalem (see 19:30–34). Since women ordinarily carried the water jars, there is the likelihood that Peter and John's search for a man carrying a water jar was the result of prior planning and agreement upon a pre-arranged signal. Perhaps Jesus knew he was being watched or perhaps he suspected Judas. Therefore Jesus took precautions in order to be sure he could complete the celebration of the Passover meal with the twelve.

The Last Supper, 22:14–23

Throughout the Third Gospel we have seen Jesus eating with many people—in the homes of Simon's mother-in-law (4:38–39) and Martha (10:38–42), in the habitations of tax collectors (5:29–30 and 19:1–10), in the homes of the Pharisees (7:36–50 and 14:1–24), in the eating places of the outcasts (15:1–3) and in the outdoors with crowds of people (9:10–17). Now, as the time of Passover begins, Jesus takes his place at the table with his chosen apostles (22:14; see 6:12–16).

Only Luke tells us of Jesus' strong desire "to eat this Passover meal *with you* before I suffer" (22:15). This verse, together with Jesus' instruction, "Go and get the Passover meal ready for *us* to eat" (22:8), conveys the conviction that the disciples (and implicitly those who read this Gospel account) are united with Jesus in his passion, death and resurrection (see also Rom 6:3–5 and 1 Cor 11:23–26). Jesus could see the proverbial "handwriting on the wall." His days, perhaps his hours, are numbered. He had taken elaborate steps (22:7–13) to make sure he would be able to eat this meal with them before he would suffer. He knows that after this meal he will not be able to eat with them again. For him there will not be another Passover until he will celebrate it in the new age brought about by the coming of the kingdom (22:16). Thus this meal is the occasion for Jesus' farewell to his friends, and the words he speaks have a deep significance for both the present moment and the future.

Just as the feeding of the five thousand in the wilderness both looked back in history to the time under Moses when the Hebrews ate manna in the desert and ahead to Jesus' giving himself in the Eucharistic bread (9:12–16), so also Jesus' celebration of the Passover looks back to the first Passover and ahead to the future celebration of the Eucharist in the believing communities or churches. Jesus and his disciples are engaged in a ritual meal that does not simply "remember" God's liberation of his people from Egyptian slavery but brings the power of God's saving deed into the present moment. In the immediate future God will again bring salvation through Jesus' salvific death and resurrection. Afterward those who believe in Jesus will begin to celebrate a ritual meal in which they will participate in the liberating self-giving of Jesus upon the cross. In his account of the Last Supper, therefore, Luke accomplishes a twofold purpose. He writes down the tradition concerning what Jesus did during his final Passover meal and he gives us a glimpse of how the Christian communities were celebrating the Eucharist in the churches that were founded by or had had contact with Paul.

During the Passover meal four cups of wine were shared, but only two are specifically mentioned by Luke (22:17, 20). In Mark and Matthew only one sharing of the cup is mentioned. The first cup came after the opening blessing, a prayer of thanksgiving which declared, "Blessed be you, Lord our God, King of the world, who has created the fruit of the vine." After the telling of the original Passover story and the singing of Psalms 113–114, another cup was passed among the participants. Perhaps it was after this cup that Jesus looked ahead to the time he would celebrate with his disciples in the fullness of God's kingdom (22:18). Thus, Jesus' declaration that he would not drink the Passover wine again expresses his anticipation that something most significant is about to be accomplished. Jesus looked ahead to the coming of the kingdom and, some two decades later, Paul was looking ahead to the coming of Jesus:

> *This means that every time you eat this bread and drink from this cup you proclaim the Lord's death until he comes (1 Cor 11:26).*

In the Passover ritual, the host takes a piece of unleavened bread, prays the blessing, breaks the bread and gives it to the persons present. At this point Jesus identified himself with the bread he distributed, saying,

> *This is my body, which is given for you. Do this in memory of me (22:19).*

The sequence of taking, giving thanks, breaking the bread and then giving it to others is the same sequence found in both the episode of the feeding of the five thousand (9:16) and in the story of the two disciples on their journey to Emmaus, where they recognize Jesus in the breaking of the bread (24:30).

Returning to the sequence of the Passover meal, it was after the head of the household passed out the bread that the main part of the meal, including the Passover lamb, was served. When this was eaten, the host prayed a blessing and passed another cup of wine to those at table. According to Luke, it is at this moment that Jesus declared,

> *This cup is God's new covenant sealed with my blood, which is poured out for you (22:20).*

The body of Jesus "given for you" and the blood "poured out for you" represents the depth of Jesus' love and expresses the Lukan understanding of the significance of the Eucharist which the early Christians celebrated in memory of Jesus (22:19). That remembering was not merely a calling to mind of what Jesus did in the past; it was also a participation in the saving event of Jesus' last Passover, death, resurrection and ascension to the Father. On the mountain Moses and Elijah spoke with Jesus about his passing over, that is, his exodus from earthly life to life in the kingdom (9:31); in the celebration of the Eucharist those who believe in Jesus are intimately related with Jesus in his gift of self to his Father. At that last meal Jesus took the things at hand—bread and wine—and consecrated them. They are now signs of the Eucharistic presence. His presence continues in the sacrament of the Eucharist everywhere and always.

This special presence, this sacramental intimacy with Jesus, is especially connected with his declaration that the cup he gave to his disciples is "God's new covenant" (22:20). This does not mean that God has terminated his covenant with the Jewish people. The Hebrew Scriptures indicate that God had entered into a series of covenants or convenantal moments, and there is no indication that a later covenant replaced the earlier one. Noah had entered into a covenant with God (Gen 6:18; 9:8–17). Later, when Abraham and God made their covenant (Gen 15:1–21; 17:1–27), the Noahide covenant was not terminated. Neither does God's covenant with Moses (Ex 24:1–11) abbrogate the covenant with Abraham. All covenants remain valid, but each successive covenant opens up new ways for God and his people to be in relationship with one another. When God declared to Jeremiah his intention to make a new covenant with his people (Jer 31:31–34), a covenant in which he would write his law on the hearts of his people, God was calling for a new and deeper relationship between himself and his people. When Jesus declared that the cup was "God's new covenant sealed with my blood" (22:20), a new relationship, a new form of intimacy with God and Jesus' disciples, came into existence. In this new covenant there are new and unsurpassable possibilities for personal relationship with the Father, through Jesus and in the Spirit.

Judas' Betrayal Foretold, 22:21–23

After Jesus had identified himself with the bread and wine shared during the celebration of God's deliverance of the Hebrews from slavery, he sorrowfully announced that he would be betrayed by one of those who shared the Passover with him (22:21). Nevertheless, even this treachery takes place in the context of God's providence (22:22). When the apostles respond by asking each other who would do this deed (22:23), we may also see Luke's apprehension that the process of the betrayal of Jesus may continue in the Christian communities. Participation in the Eucharist was not a guarantee that all members would be faithful to Jesus and to one another.

REFLECTION. No matter how often we perform a certain activity, there will come a time when we do it for the last time. Luke wants his readers to give their complete attention to what Jesus shares with his friends during these last hours before his death. The setting is charged with deep affection and intimacy. What Jesus said then, his disciples will remember and interpret in light of his passion and resurrection. As we reflect on the desire of Jesus to share this last Passover, his words and himself with his friends, we could ask ourselves what we might say on a similar occasion. What would we want to share with spouse, children, family or friends in the face of death? In asking ourselves how we would want our loved ones to remember us on such an occasion, we will more deeply appreciate the words Jesus speaks during these final hours. We will also perceive more clearly how painful Judas' betrayal was to Jesus.

It is important to keep in mind that Luke includes two levels of meaning in his account of the Last Supper. One level deals with what Jesus did and said when he shared this final meal with his disciples. Another level relates Jesus' words and actions in terms of their significance for Luke's audience. Because of the inspired nature of Christian Scriptures we are included in that audience. We may ask ourselves about our own quality of participation in the celebration of the Eucharist. The Second Vatican Council's *Constitution on the Sacred Liturgy* points out that our participation in the Eucharist is most effective when we come to celebrate "with proper dispositions," when our "thoughts match" our words, and when we "cooperate with divine grace" (art. 11). The Constitution also asks pastors to be aware of their responsibility to plan for and preside over the Eucharist in such a way "that the faithful take part knowingly, actively, and fruitfully" (art. 11). These words have many implications for parish councils, liturgy commissions, adult education teams, parents, clergy, directors of religious education, principals and catechists teaching in both schools and CCD programs. Through our graced efforts others may come to appreciate more deeply the command of Jesus, "Do this in memory of me" (22:19).

There is a twofold dimension to the affirmation we make when we receive the Eucharist and say "Amen" to the words, "The body of Christ." First, each of us receives the risen Jesus in the consecrated bread; second, our personal relationship with the other members of the community is deepened. This is so because sanctifying grace is a relationship with God rather than an object given by God to each individual. Grace is a relationship of faith and love between Father, Son, Holy Spirit and believer, and this relationship includes all persons who are in relationship with the Father through the Son and in the Spirit. Since the whole Church is the body of Christ, any deepening of our love-relationship with Jesus is also a deepening of the union we have with his people. Thus to love Jesus more fervently goes hand in hand with deeper commitment to his body, the community we call "Church."

The Mass is not an event in which the laity are spectators. As baptized members of the community we come to Sunday worship for the basic purpose of offering, along with the priest, the gift of the risen Christ to the Father. The most significant gift we can offer is God's own Son. But when we offer this gift, we also offer the gift of our very own selves, for we are the body of Christ; we are united with Jesus through baptism. Thus this act of offering Jesus and ourselves is the answer to the question Catholics often ask, "Why do we go to mass each Sunday?" We come to Sunday worship for the purpose of offering the whole body of Christ to God. We come together as a community to offer ourselves individually and communally with Jesus to our Father.

The Argument About Greatness, 22:24–30

COMMENTARY. Verses 24 to 27 link the betrayal of Jesus with the desire for power and authority. According to Mark 10:42–45, this incident concerning the seeking of recognition and prestige takes place on the journey to Jerusalem. Luke, however, places Jesus' teaching regarding the importance of serving others in the setting of the Last Supper. Because Luke places this "word" of Jesus in this solemn context, we can see that Luke is stressing the value of humble service of others. This is another indication of the reversal theme. The "common sense" value lies in ranking one's importance in terms of the kind of service one commands, while Jesus urges the leaders of his community to imitate himself in his role as the "one who serves" (24:27). In sum, Jesus reminds the apostles that in the community of his disciples greatness will not be manifested in terms of power (as among the pagans), but will be measured in terms of the quality and wholeheartedness of one's service.

That service, because it is modeled upon Jesus' example, will unite the apostles with the trials of Jesus (22:28). The apostles' fidelity to Jesus will culminate in receiving from Jesus what he has received from his Father: a place at the table in the kingdom (22:29–30a). They will also share in Jesus' authority since they will rule the twelve tribes of Israel (22:30b). There is an apocalyptic or end-time flavor to this promise, which looks ahead to the time of ultimate judgment. Earlier in the Third Gospel Jesus made a similar promise in the context of selling everything in order to have riches in heaven: "Do not be afraid, little flock, for your Father is pleased to give you the Kingdom" (12:32ff).

Jesus Foresees Peter's Denial and Repentance, 22:31–34

Mark and Matthew situate the prophecy of Peter's denial after Jesus and the apostles have left the upper room. Luke, however, places this scene in the context of the Last Supper. Thus Peter's denial, his subsequent repentance and Jesus' readiness to forgive are associated with the Eucharist.

The seriousness of what Jesus is about to say is reflected in his repetition of Simon's name and the command to listen (22:31). The setting for Peter's denial and repentance has cosmic dimensions. God has given Satan permission to test severely the faith of Peter and *all* the others (22:31). Satan may have succeeded with Judas (22:3), but

Jesus declares that he has prayed for Simon with the expressed intention that Peter's faith will not fail (22:32a). In the context of Luke's account, the faith of Peter is summed up in his declaration, "You are God's Messiah" (9:20). This is a time of interior crisis, for Satan is at work trying to separate Peter and the others from Jesus. But Jesus' prayer prevails. Although Peter will say that he does not know Jesus (22:57–60), Peter never denies that Jesus is God's Messiah. Thus, even though he does deny being a disciple of Jesus, Peter's faith does not fail in the most crucial dimension.

When Jesus next states that, after Peter's turning back, he must strengthen the brothers (22:32b), we see a greater stress placed on Peter's repentance than on his momentary denial. In this context, the strengthening of his brothers refers to the crucial importance of bearing witness that Jesus is God's Messiah. It is possible that "the brothers" refers to all future believers whose faith will be authentic to the extent that it is linked with the faith of Peter who believed that Jesus is God's Messiah. There is also strength to be found in Peter's example. He had his human weakness, but after he had sinned, he repented and returned to Jesus. For those Christians who would deny Jesus under the threat of loss of property, health or even life itself, they could find the courage to turn back to Jesus and return to the community, for even the great Peter had done the same. This passage (22:31–32) has significant links with Peter's profession of faith in Matthew 16:16–19. Jesus declares that Peter with his faith in Jesus as the Messiah is the rock on which the Church will be built.

While Peter responds to Jesus' prophecy by declaring that he would suffer prison and death with Jesus, by the next morning Peter will have declared three times that he did not know Jesus (22:33–34).

Preparation for Crisis, 22:35–38

This unit begins (22:35) with Jesus' recalling the disciples' experience when they were sent out on mission and were given all they needed (10:3ff). Now, however, circumstances are very different. Opposition faces Jesus at every turn, and what happens to Jesus will also be the portion of his followers. Citing the fourth suffering servant poem (Is 53:12), Jesus interprets this passage in terms of his own death (22:37). To stress the need for preparedness and strength on the part of his followers, Jesus uses the first century metaphors of purse and sword (22:36). The disciples, however, once again misunderstood their Master and show Jesus their two swords (22:38). They have taken his words literally. Exasperated with their failure to understand his metaphorical language, Jesus brings an end to the dialogue by declaring, "That is enough!" Later, on the Mount of Olives, Jesus will rebuke one of the disciples who attempts to protect him by means of the sword. "Enough of this!" (22:51) Jesus will say, echoing his response to the disciples who had brought forth their two swords as an example of their preparedness (22:38).

Week Eight

The final portion of this study of the Third Gospel begins with Jesus' prayer on the Mount of Olives and concludes with Jesus' ascension to his Father. It seems as if the power of darkness is in charge of the events that take place—Jesus is betrayed, arrested, falsely accused and unjustly condemned to crucifixion.

But throughout his trial, passion and death Jesus continues to manifest in deeds the teachings he had proclaimed during his ministry. He forgives his enemies, endures betrayal, ministers to sinners, expresses compassion for others and accepts whatever comes as an expression of his Father's will leading to the salvation of all.

As Jesus hangs on the cross Luke connects the pains and insults endured by Jesus with the theme of the suffering servant as it was manifested during the temptations in the desert (4:1–13). Different people witness the crucifixion of Jesus with different attitudes, some reviling him, others asking for forgiveness or declaring his innocence. His disciples watch from a distance.

On Easter Sunday the women find the empty tomb, the two disciples on the way to Emmaus encounter Jesus in the breaking of the bread, Peter declares: "The Lord is risen," and all the disciples are addressed by the risen Jesus who commissions them to go as witnesses to all nations. As official witnesses these disciples stand behind the "orderly account" that Luke has written for Theophilus for the purpose of his knowing "the full truth about everything" which he has been taught (1:3–4).

DAILY STUDY ASSIGNMENTS: WEEK EIGHT

Day	Luke	Commentary
1	22:39–71	pp. 234–240
2	23:1–25	pp. 240–246
3	23:26–56	pp. 246–253
4	24:1–35	pp. 253–261
5	24:36–53	pp. 261–266

6 Review Luke 22:39—24:53 in light of the questions for reflection listed below.

7 Group meets for study and sharing.

1. Compare Luke 22:40–46 with 11:2–4. What are the similarities between Jesus' prayer on the Mount of Olives and the prayer he taught his disciples?

2. Which event of the Lucan passion narrative is most personally significant for you?

3. No one wants to carry the cross. How has Luke tried to give us the courage to do so in the way he has recounted the passion, death and resurrection of Jesus?

4. What connections does Luke make between the passion narrative in 23:35–43 and Jesus' temptations in 4:1–12?

5. How does the Exodus theme in 9:30–31 relate to Jesus' words in 24:25–27?

6. The road to Emmaus might signify that discouragement or temptation which leads one away from following Je-

sus. What might correspond to the "road to Emmaus" in your life? How might the breaking of the bread strengthen you so that you can live in hope?

7. Some commentators see a summation of Luke's account of the Gospel in the words of Jesus in 24:45–48. Which major themes in Luke's account can you find in these verses?

Jesus Prays on the Mount of Olives, 22:39–46

OVERVIEW. The story of Jesus' passion, resurrection and ascension is the climax of Luke's account of the Gospel. The account of the sufferings and death of Jesus was the first part of the tradition about Jesus to be written down. No other aspect of the life of Jesus has been handed down to us with such detail. This is most appropriate since the passion account, along with the proclamation of the resurrection, was the focal point of the preaching of the apostles and the early missionaries.

For the most part Luke follows Mark 14:1—15:47, but he has also added information from other sources in such a way that his major themes stand out clearly. Thus Jesus is the innocent martyr who goes to his death forgiving all those who have brought him to the cross. He is the model for all those who, like Simon of Cyrene, would follow after him. The passion and death of Jesus is a summary of the way he lived. He suffered with the perception that God's will was somehow being manifested, and therefore he accepted in trust the tragic and painful circumstances of his death. Throughout the Third Gospel God's power has been manifest in Jesus' teaching, healings and exorcisms. In Jesus' death upon the cross we see the culmination of God's wonderful deeds on behalf of the salvation of all people.

COMMENTARY. After the supper Jesus leads his disciples to the Mount of Olives. Long before, when his followers asked Jesus for a specific prayer to express their identity as disciples, Jesus taught them how to address their heavenly Father. This prayer concluded with the petition to be spared from temptation (11:4). On the Mount of Olives Jesus twice tells his disciples: "Pray that you will not fall into temptation" (22:40, 46). Because this admonition to pray brackets the entire scene, we can see that it states the main concern of this section. Jesus exemplifies the relationship between prayer and "hard testing" (see 11:4). Everything in this scene is indicative of the struggle Jesus is going through. In the immediate future he faces humiliation and pain. The stress is so severe that Jesus asks that the suffering might somehow be taken away, but, nevertheless, he chooses that his Father's will be accomplished no matter the cost to him (22:42). The intensity of Jesus' struggle, so expressive of the humanity that he shares with us all, is indicated in the sustaining presence of an angel and in the reference to his sweat "like drops of blood falling to the ground" (22:43-44). Jesus undergoes the deepest kind of psychological distress.

Returning to his disciples, he finds them asleep (22:45). Luke adds the explanation that they were "worn out by grief" (22:45). Jesus encourages them to pray so that they will not yield to temptation (22:46). Jesus has provided the example. He has prayed, struggled in his time of trial, and faced what is now inevitable: death at the hands of his enemies. Having united his will with the will of his Father, Jesus, the innocent servant, faces his martyrdom. His prayer has enabled him to conquer the fear of death. With this bitter conflict of heart and will resolved, Jesus will endure the trial, scourging and crucifixion with that particular serenity of the person who knows that his life is in the hands of God.

The Arrest of Jesus, 22:47-53

Verses 47 and 48 speak of the terrible nature of Judas' betrayal. The crowd that comes for Jesus is led by Judas, described as "one of the twelve disciples." As Judas approaches, Jesus asks him if it is his intention to betray the Son of Man "with a kiss." The kiss is a sign of affection and friendship; to use this gesture in betrayal indicates the depth of Judas' decision to turn against Jesus.

When Jesus' disciples grasp what is happening, they take out their two swords (see 22:38) and, without waiting for a reply to their question, one of the disciples attacks and injures the slave of the high priest (22:49–50). Only Luke records that Jesus rebuked his disciple and healed the man's ear (22:51). Note the miracle theme that is brought to this scene by Luke. In the beginning of his ministry, Jesus' power to perform such works had drawn the disciples to Jesus (see 4:38–41; 5:1–11). That same power is present in this hour of great trial and it is used as it always has been used—to heal others.

In Mark's account Jesus is seized before this attack on the slave; in Luke it is only after Jesus forbids any more resistance ("Enough of this!") that he is arrested. Having been apprehended, Jesus faces his captors and asks them why they have come armed with swords and clubs as if to arrest an outlaw (22:52). When Jesus points out that they did not attempt to arrest him in the temple, the irony in his question manifests itself. Had he been an outlaw, they would have arrested him publicly, not at night in a deserted place.

Among his captors are not only soldiers and officers of the temple guard, but also the chief priests and elders (22:52). These leaders, in concert with Judas, seem to triumph as "the power of darkness rules" (22:53). Their rule will be brief. In the remainder of the Third Gospel Judas will not be seen again. There are two traditions about his death. According to Matthew 27:5, Judas hanged himself. In another tradition Judas bought a field with the money he received for betraying Jesus; in this field Judas fell and died (see Acts 1:18–19).

Peter Denies Jesus, 22:54–62

Peter, while never saying that Jesus is not the Messiah, seems to have so feared for his safety that he declared that he did not know Jesus (22:57), that he was not a disciple (22:58) and that he did not understand what was at issue concerning Jesus (22:60). After Jesus was arrested, Peter "followed at a distance" (22:54). To follow Jesus is to be a disciple. To follow Jesus "at a distance" makes one a timid disciple. Peter knows that Jesus is God's Messiah, but he does not yet realize that Jesus is the suffering Messiah. This revelation into the full nature of Jesus' Messiahship will take place when the risen Jesus opens the minds of his disciples so that they can understand the Scriptures (see 24:45).

As the rooster crowed, Jesus looked at Peter, thus bringing to Peter's mind what Jesus had said during the Passover meal (22:34). Overwhelmed by what he has done, Peter weeps bitterly. Unlike Judas, Peter is able to repent, to turn back to Jesus. Neither Peter nor any of the other disciples are directly associated with Jesus in any aspect of the trial, passion and death. But Luke indicates that Peter and the disciples were there among "all those who knew Jesus personally" as they "stood at a distance" watching him die on the cross (23:49).

Jesus Is Beaten and Brought Before the Council, 22:63–71

While Peter went away weeping bitterly (22:62), those guarding Jesus began to abuse him. For some time between the coming of night and the break of day, Jesus' guards insulted and beat him, making a parody of his prophetic teaching by hitting him while blindfolded and then asking him to identify each of his tormentors (22:63–65).

Luke's account of the trial of Jesus by the Sanhedrin differs from Mark's. Luke tells us nothing about the "witnesses" who reported Jesus' statements about the destruction and the rebuilding of the temple (Mk 14:57–61). There is no mention of the Sanhedrin's charge of blasphemy against Jesus nor the passing of the death verdict upon Jesus (Mk 14:64). According to Luke there is only one early morning meeting of the council, whereas Mark reports two meetings, one taking place at night (Mk 14:53–65) and the other in the morning (Mk 15:1). This is another indication that the evangelists have passed on traditions which were not a stenographer's courtroom transcript. What we read in verses 66 through 71 is a combination of historical memories, some indication of why Jesus was handed over to Pilate, and a profession of the Christian community's belief in the divinity of Jesus.

Having been arrested at night and then confined in the home of the high priest (22:54), Jesus is brought before the council of the Sanhedrin in the morning (22:66). It seems to have been a hastily convened meeting. According to Luke the meeting was attended by "the elders, the chief priests, and the teachers of the Law" (22:66). These are the same parties mentioned in Jesus' first prophecy of his passion: "The Son of Man must suffer much and be rejected by the elders, the chief priests, and the teachers of the Law" (9:22).

The question "Are you the Messiah?" serves to provide a context for the passion narrative. During the ministry of Jesus, the title of Messiah was not crucial to his mission and identity. Jesus had publicly avoided this title because it was so likely to be misunderstood in terms of his being a nationalistic political figure. However, his teaching and his actions, particularly his triumphant entry into Jerusalem (19:34–40) and his driving the merchants out of the temple (19:45–46), led many to suspect that Jesus was claiming a messianic role. Thus, Jesus does not answer directly the question put to him by the council. The fact is that he did see his mission in terms of being God's Messiah, but a Messiah far different than the people expected. Jesus' reply in 22:68 may indicate that he is the Messiah but not according to their idea of a political Messiah.

Note the literary parallelism that Luke gives us. Just as a discussion of the meaning of Jesus' messiahship was followed by a declaration from Jesus about the Son of Man in 9:18–22, so at the trial the discussion about Jesus' identity as Messiah is followed by the statement that "the Son of man will be seated at the right side of Almighty God" (22:69). The statement could mean that Jesus would soon be vindicated by his exaltation from death or it could mean that Jesus is identifying himself with the power of God. The members of the Sanhedrin ask Jesus if he is making himself equal to God, and Jesus' reply, "You say that I am," seems to be an indirect admission of his divine identity. (This reflects the faith of the believing community that Jesus is identified with the nature of God.) The council, like all Jews, were not expecting a divine Messiah. They would have been more likely to understand the title, "Son of God," in the sense of the Hebrew Scriptures which spoke

of the children of David as God's sons (2 Sam 7:14) and
which referred to God's Davidic King as "my son" (Ps 2:7).
Because the titles attributed to Jesus during the hearing
("the Christ" and "the Son of God") were most likely
understood as messianic claims by the assembled priests,
elders and scribes, they have all they need to bring charges
against Jesus. In accordance with popular expectations, the
Messiah would also be a king, a political leader. With Jesus'
admission as evidence, they take Jesus to Pilate (23:1).

Jesus Before Pilate, 23:1–5

Luke seems to be more concerned about Pilate's role
in the crucifixion of Jesus than the role of the Sanhedrin.
Writing for the local churches in the eastern portion of the
Empire, Luke wants to demonstrate that the followers of
Jesus are not a threat to the stability of the political order.
Thus, three times Pilate declares that Jesus is innocent
(23:4, 14 and 22).

The Sanhedrin brings Jesus to Pilate. Three charges
are made against their prisoner, each of them having some
basis in fact. First, Jesus is accused of misleading the people (23:2). Note that Jesus is not charged with insurrection.
In the eyes of his accusers Jesus had "misled" the people
by interpreting the law in ways that differed with the established doctrines of the Pharisees and the teachers of the
law; he criticized many aspects of the social system of his
day and he stressed the ideal of humble service in contrast
to a social order which valued wealth and power. The second charge springs from the attempt to trap Jesus regarding the coin of tribute (20:20–26). Although Jesus left the
question of paying taxes to Caesar open-ended by declaring "Pay to the Emperor what belongs to the Emperor,"

here he is falsely accused of telling the people not to pay taxes. The most damaging charge is the third, based on the fact that Jesus did not deny that he was God's anointed Messiah. The council clarifies for Pilate the meaning of Christ (the Anointed One), that is, "king" (23:2).

When Pilate asks Jesus if the third charge is true, Jesus gives a non-committal reply (23:3). Pilate takes this as a denial of the charge and declares that Jesus does not deserve condemnation (23:4). This leads his accusers to vigorously assert that Jesus' teaching has stirred up violence from Galilee to Judea, thus providing Pilate with an opportunity to spare himself the effort of making a decision. Pilate sends Jesus to Herod, the administrator of Galilee (23:6–7).

Herod, who has long been curious about Jesus (see 9:9), is pleased about the turn of events that brings the Galilean miracle worker into his power (23:8). However, when Jesus answers neither his questions nor the accusations of the chief priests and Pharisees, Herod and his soldiers treat him with contempt and then send him back to Pilate (23:9–10). Luke, the only evangelist to record this incident of Jesus' being shunted between Pilate and Herod, again provides a secular ruler's testimony regarding the innocence of Jesus. Herod treated Jesus like a fool, not a criminal, and then sent him back to Pilate, thereby befriending the Roman governor by acknowledging his higher authority (22:12).

Jesus Is Sentenced to Death, 23:13–25

Luke structures his account of the trial of Jesus in three segments. In the first section Pilate calls together priests, leaders and people in order to tell them the outcome of Herod's judgment. Recalling that he had already ques-

tioned Jesus and had found no reason to condemn him
(23:4), Pilate informs the accusers of Jesus that Herod has
concurred in his own assessment of the innocence of Jesus
(23:14–15). However, in an attempt to appease the group
of Jewish plaintiffs, Pilate declares his intention to have Jesus whipped before he is set free (23:16).

In the second section of Jesus' trial (23:18–23), the accusers of Jesus have the center stage. They want Jesus
dead. Since Pilate had spoken of freeing Jesus, the group
of Jews demand that if anyone is set free, let him be Bar-
rabas (23:18). When Pilate again appealed to the Jewish
leaders and the people they had assembled, they all cry out
for Jesus' crucifixion. This is the first instance in the Third
Gospel in which the word "crucify" is used. Since death by
crucifixion was punishment for a political or secular crime
against the Roman Empire, Pilate, for the third time, declares that Jesus is innocent (23:22). Pilate's pledge to have
Jesus whipped and then let go still fails to change the
minds of those demanding Jesus' crucifixion; the crowd
then gets what it wanted (23:23).

In the third section (23:24–25), Pilate delivers the death
sentence wanted by the Jewish leaders. Earlier they had
handed Jesus over to Pilate; now Pilate hands Jesus over to
the same group of Jewish leaders by yielding to their demands. The innocence of Jesus is heightened by the release
of the man guilty of riot and murder (23:25). It is noteworthy that Luke makes no reference to the scourging of Jesus.
Luke does not heavily lay the blame for the death of Jesus
on Pilate. Out of delicacy or deference to the Roman governor, Luke omits Pilate's ordering of the scourging of an
innocent man. Although it was Pilate alone who had the
authority to crucify Jesus and it was Pilate alone who de-
livered the verdict of death, Luke downplays the role of

Roman authority in the death of Jesus. Noting that Luke has placed much stress on mercy and forgiveness in his account of the good news, it is in keeping with Luke's approach that he tends to diminish the guilt of all those responsible for the death of Jesus.

REFLECTION. Who were those mainly responsible for bringing Jesus to Pilate and what was their motivation? In all four of the Gospel accounts we find glimpses of why the enemies of Jesus wanted him dead. Scholars have pointed out that the Judaism of Jesus' day was a pluralistic religion which was made up of various religious groups such as the Sadducees, the Essenes, the Zealots and the Pharisees.

Most of the power or political leverage which the Jewish people had under the Romans was exercised by the Sadducees. They were well-to-do. The priests, who came from their ranks, controlled the temple. To a large extent their way of life hinged on cooperation with Roman rule. For example, the chief priest could hold office only if permission was given by Rome.

From the point of view of the Sadducees, any threat to the status quo was a threat to them because it could lead to a change in the delicate relationship they had with the Roman government. A man like Jesus, having much popular support (see Lk 19:47–48), would be perceived as dangerous. When Jesus drove the merchants out of the temple precincts, he was calling for a radical change in the religious attitudes of the people (19:45–46). Those who had most to fear in the presence and activity of Jesus would have been the Sadducees. They would most likely be the ones who would want to see Jesus dead.

It seems that the Sadducees took the lead in pressing for the death of Jesus. Luke records that Judas "went off and spoke with the chief priests and the officers of the temple guard about how he could betray Jesus to them" (22:4). It was the Sadducees who controlled the temple guard, and it was the chief priests, elders and officers of the temple guard who took Jesus prisoner on the Mount of Olives (22:52). Putting the pieces of information together, we see this pattern: some Jewish leaders, particularly the Sadducees, were committed to protecting their interests by ridding themselves of anyone perceived as a threat. They seized Jesus when the time was right for them, held a hearing, and brought Jesus to Pilate. This brings us to a second question: What was Pilate's role in the death of Jesus?

Jesus was brought before Pilate and accused of misleading the people, speaking against the payment of taxes and claiming that he was the Messiah, a king (23:2). It is the political charge that concerned Pilate (23:3). Jesus was accused of sedition. Death by crucifixion was punishment reserved for slaves, pirates and insurrectionists. Luke has omitted the allegations that Jesus said he would destroy the temple or that he was guilty of blasphemy (see Mk 14:57–65; Mt 26:60–66). For Luke, the sole consideration was Jesus' Messiahship. He points out how reluctant Pilate was to condemn an innocent man (23:4–25). It is characteristic of Luke to stress the themes of mercy, forgiveness and reconciliation. Perhaps Luke did not want to lay the blame for Jesus' death on anyone. Perhaps Luke wanted to portray Pilate, placed in his position by the Roman Empire, in the kindest possible light. It is notable that all four accounts of the Gospel tend to portray Pilate as a reluctant participant in an event not totally in his control. However, history records that he ruled as a tyrant. Even though the evangelists are generally silent about the harshness of Pilate's rule, there is this fleeting glimpse of the dark side of his character:

At that time some people were there who told Jesus about the Galileans whom Pilate had killed while they were offering sacrifices to God (Lk 13:1).

Pilate, obsessed by the possibility of a Jewish revolt against Roman rule, killed many. He sentenced numerous Jewish citizens to death by crucifixion. Few had the benefit of trial. So, on the one hand, Luke represents Pilate as a governor personally convinced of the innocence of Jesus, but reluctantly yielding to the demands of some people and some Jewish leaders. On the other hand, Luke makes it clear that Pilate alone had the authority to set Jesus free or have him crucified (23:16, 22, 24). From all indications, Jesus was put to death because Pontius Pilate sentenced him to crucifixion for the crime of sedition against the Roman state.

The plot of a few Jewish leaders, aided by Judas, had succeeded. They had accused Jesus of sedition, and Pilate found it expedient to have Jesus executed. What should be our attitude toward those who were guilty of Jesus' murder? First we should take into account Luke's inspired perspective. He tells us that Jesus himself forgave all those involved in his death (23:34). Luke then goes on to record the total context of God's plans: it was necessary that Jesus pass through suffering and death in order to enter into his glory (24:26, 46–47). The teaching of the Catholic Church on this matter is this:

> *True, authorities of the Jews and those who followed their lead pressed for the death of Jesus (cf. Jn 19:6); still, what happened in his passion cannot be blamed upon all the Jews then living, without distinction, nor upon the Jews of today. Although the Church is the new people of God, the Jews should not be presented as repudiated or cursed by God, as if such views followed from the Holy Scripture (Declaration on the*

Relationship of the Church to Non-Christian Religions, art. 4).

As Cardinal Koenig summarized the issue, those either historically accountable or historically involved in the death of Jesus were a single Roman governor, a handful of Jesus' own people, and a number of soldiers from the tenth cohort of the Roman army then stationed in Palestine. They were all forgiven by Jesus from the cross (Lk 23:34).

Jesus Is Crucified, 23:26–43

COMMENTARY. With Jesus condemned to death, Luke now recounts the very last portion of Jesus' earthly journey, the way from Jerusalem to his Father. As Jesus makes his journey, he models those attitudes his followers are called to express in their own lives.

Persons condemned to crucifixion usually carried the crossbeam to the place of execution. Jesus was so weakened that the soldiers conscripted Simon of Cyrene to carry the crossbeam the rest of the way. While Mark simply stated this fact (Mk 15:21), Luke added the significant detail that Simon carried the cross "behind Jesus" (23:26). Simon thus becomes a symbol of the Christian disciple, the follower to whom Jesus addresses the words, "If anyone wants to come with me, he must forget himself, take up his cross everyday, and follow me" (9:23).

Behind Jesus and Simon are many people. The crowd is depicted as being more sympathetic than hostile. Among the people are some mourning women (23:27). These women ministered to condemned prisoners by offering pain-killing opiates to lessen their agonies. Jesus addresses them with compassionate and prophetic words. They are the ones who should weep for themselves because of the devastation that will come because Jerusalem did not recognize the time of its salvation (see 19:41–44). When the days of trial arrive, the barren women will consider themselves more fortunate than the mothers, for the barren will not have to watch their own sons and daughters suffer and die. Jesus tells them to have sorrow for themselves then, a time when they will wish for an earthquake to bury them rather than live (23:30). The reason Jesus gives takes the form of a proverb: if green wood burns, then how much the more will the dry wood blaze (23:31)? If the Romans treat the innocent Jesus as a rebel, what terrible things will the Romans do when Jerusalem actually revolts against Rome?

Two criminals are crucified with Jesus (23:32–33). As Jesus is nailed to the cross, he prays for those involved in his crucifixion, asking his Father to forgive them for what they are doing out of ignorance (23:34). Of the four evangelists only Luke records this prayer in which Jesus forgives his enemies. Thus Jesus faces his death with the same attitudes which filled his life. Luke wants us to perceive Jesus as the innocent one who lived his life doing God's will (2:49), who spent his ministry serving the poor, the crippled, the blind and the lame (see 14:13, 21), and who taught both the unlearned and the scholars. At his crucifixion Jesus encounters the darkness of the human heart and transcends that darkness by prayerfully forgiving those who are taking away his life. The words of Jesus recall the final lines of the fourth suffering servant poem:

My devoted servant, with whom I am pleased, will bear the punishment of many and for his sake I will forgive them. . . .

He willingly gave his life and shared the fate of evil men. He took the place of many sinners and prayed that they might be forgiven (Is 53:11–12).

It was the custom for soldiers to take the clothes of those who were crucified, for the property of those guilty of sedition was forfeited to the state (23:34b). Psalm 22 (verse 18), "They gamble for my clothes and divide them among themselves," becomes one of the Psalms fulfilled by Jesus (see 24:44).

As the soldiers cast dice for Jesus' clothing, the people "stood there watching" while the Jewish leaders ridicule Jesus (23:35). Luke wants to contrast the passive attitude of the crowd with the scorn directed at Jesus by the leaders of the people. The taunts of the leaders, "He saved others; let him save himself if he is the Messiah whom God has chosen" (23:35), echo the wording of Satan's tempting in the desert: "If you are God's Son, order this stone to turn into bread. . . . If you are God's Son, throw yourself down from here" (4:3, 9). Jesus' enemies ask for a miraculous descent from the cross—as if they might believe in a sign through which Jesus would save himself. At stake here is the same issue that is found in the temptation of Jesus in the desert (4:1–13) as well as elsewhere in Jesus' ministry: What kind of Messiah is Jesus? Does Jesus come to be the Messiah of power and success or does he come to be the suffering servant of God who reveals that salvation is a matter of losing one's life in order to be saved by the power of God (see 9:24; 17:33)? Jesus is "the Messiah God has chosen" (see 2:26; 3:22; 24:46).

The soldiers repeat the mockery of the Jewish leaders, referring to Jesus in terms of the criminal charge attached to the cross: "Save yourself if you are the king of the Jews!" (23:36–37). But Jesus has come to save others by losing his own life. The offering of cheap wine, perhaps an allusion to Psalm 69:21, is part of the soldiers' mockery of Jesus. Of the four evangelists, only Luke tells us of the words spoken by those crucified with Jesus (13:39–43). While one of the criminals joins in the insults directed at Jesus, the second criminal testifies to Jesus' innocence by pointing out that their sentences are deserved whereas Jesus "has done no wrong" (23:40–41). The second criminal, by referring to the fear of God, recognizes that both he and his partner are the ones under God's judgment. The very recognition of one's sins is indicative of repentance. Then, turning to Jesus, the dying man makes an act of faith in Jesus as the suffering Messiah: "Remember me, Jesus, when you come as King!" (23:42).

When Jesus replies, "I promise you that today you will be in Paradise with me" (23:43), he does once more what he had done all during his ministry: "The Son of Man came to seek and to save the lost" (19:10; see also 15:1–2, 7, 10). When Jesus declares that the dying man "will be . . . with me," Jesus makes him a disciple even as he dies. The criminal had asked only that Jesus remember him "when you come as King." But Jesus promises him immediate salvation. The stress on the present moment, "*Today* you will be in Paradise with me," recalls a similar emphasis on the present moment found in the angels' joyful proclamation to the shepherds: "*This very day* . . . your Savior was born—Christ the Lord!" (2:11).

The Death of Jesus, 23:44–49

As Jesus hangs on the cross Luke notes that darkness covered the land until the hour Jesus died. This may be connected with the words Jesus spoke at the time of his arrest: ". . . this is your hour to act, when the power of darkness rules" (22:53). Along with the sign of extraordinary darkness Luke tells of another portent, the tearing in two of the curtain that separated the holy of holies (the sacred place of God's special presence) from the holy place where the people worshiped in the temple (23:45). The rending of the curtain may signify that God's special presence is no longer to be found in the temple but in the crucified and risen Jesus, or it may symbolize the approaching destruction of the temple in 70 A.D.

Luke does not record Jesus' anguished praying of Psalm 22:1, "My God, my God, why did you abandon me?" (Mk 15:34). Addressing his last words to his Father, Jesus cries out with the words of Psalm 31:5, "Father! In your hands I place my spirit!" (23:46). Then Jesus died. By his prayer he died as he lived, trusting in his Father. Between the two criminals he died as he lived, being present to the sinners and outcasts for whom he came. His death expressed a total correspondence with the values he taught and the attitudes by which he lived. The "power of darkness" (22:53) appears to have its rule, but Jesus is the one who has triumphed. He has overcome the evil of those who took away his life—by forgiving his murders and then offering his life to God. Thus the army officer, witnessing what Jesus has done, praises God and declares, "Certainly he was a good man!" (23:47). The praise of God is Luke's favorite manner of indicating a person's response to a revelation of God's power. Thus the Roman officer bears witness to the martyrdom of an innocent man.

Luke next records the reaction of the people to the death of Jesus. Having seen Jesus hang on the cross and die, they return to their homes beating their breasts to express their grief for the executed Jesus (23:48). The expression of sorrow could also be a manifestation of contrition for whatever involvement they may have had in the death of Jesus. (Luke has noted that "the chief priests, the leaders, and *the people*" had asked for the death of Jesus in verses 13, 18, 21 and 23.)

The last group of persons who saw Jesus die is made up of "all those who knew Jesus personally" (23:49). They were off in the distance, away from Jesus' enemies. While they may have feared being too closely related to Jesus (Peter denied that he knew Jesus), they have not broken their relationship with him. The women who had followed Jesus from Galilee are singled out (see 8:2–3) to stress the continuity of the witnessing to Jesus, particularly among the women who will soon be called to be witnesses to Jesus' resurrection (see 23:55 and 24:1–7). Regarding the apostles, the eleven are included even though Satan has tried to test them as farmer separates the wheat from the chaff (22:32). Satan has not succeeded. The prayer of Jesus that Peter's faith will not fail has been answered. Although Peter lost his nerve, he never lost faith by denying that Jesus is the Messiah.

REFLECTION. Each of us will someday have the opportunity to pray as Jesus prayed: "Father! In your hands I place my spirit!" Our own dying does not have to be something that merely happens to us. It can be also our own action, our own handing ourselves over to our Father in trusting faith. It could be the most personal act of worship anyone of us could make, since it has the potential for being our most complete act of self-giving. Each one of us can resolve to follow Jesus in this way.

It is important to realize that Jesus did not recklessly disregard the value of his life. Only with great reluctance did Jesus accept his death: "Father, if you will, take this cup of suffering away from me" (22:42). He recoiled from the idea of being killed. Possessing the same humanity as we do, Jesus did not want to die. Indeed, life is a great gift, and as such it is only reluctantly surrendered no matter what the cause or reason.

It follows that it is not Christian virtue to depreciate the gift of life, or to devalue it because eternal life is so much more desirable. On the contrary, death is the giving up of that which is deeply meaningful. It is not Christian piety to scoff at the life we have, or to consider it merely a burdensome chore to live out our allotted years. According to Jesus' prayer on the Mount of Olives, Jesus valued his human life so dearly that he wanted to be spared the agony of suffering and death. He laid down his life with the same reluctance we feel, for he was like us in all things but sin. He did submit to death, but only for values that transcended the goodness of life, namely, fidelity to his loving commitment to his Father and his love for others.

The death of Jesus can lead us to appreciate the gift of life we are given in the present moment. The more we can be grateful for what it means to live as a human person, the more we can enter into solidarity with the whole human family, particularly with our brothers and sisters who are poor, oppressed or in any way cheated of their human dignity. If we truly love life, if we recognize what human life meant to Jesus, then we can find in this recognition the motivation to reach out to other members of the human family so that they may find life a blessing as much as we. It is true that we all are the world; we all are the children waiting and hoping for a better day; we all yearn for a more human way of living.

The Burial of Jesus, 23:50–56

COMMENTARY. The scene shifts from the place of crucifixion to the palace of Pilate where Joseph of Arimathea requests permission to remove the body of Jesus from the cross. Joseph acts to prevent the body of Jesus from being buried with the criminals in a common grave. Thus Pilate's granting of the request (23:52–53) is another attestation of Jesus' innocence.

Since it was late Friday afternoon when Jesus was taken down from the cross, Jesus' body seems to have been placed in the tomb without the accustomed spices and perfumes. For this reason the women from Galilee accompany Joseph to the burial place so that they know where to go with the ointments and spices on the day following the sabbath (23:55–56). As the women ready the spices at the end of Friday, the day of preparation, they do not realize that the sabbath itself is about to become the day of preparation for the resurrection of Jesus.

The Women and the Empty Tomb, 24:1–12

OVERVIEW. When we compare the reports of the resurrection of Jesus, we find that there are many more differences between the four evangelists here than in the passion accounts. The details of the passion narrative were publicly witnessed by many; the experience of the risen Jesus was rooted in faith.

The most obvious difference in the accounts of the resurrection of Jesus is the location of the appearances of the risen Jesus to the eleven apostles. Luke and the twentieth chapter of John situate the appearances of Jesus in the city of Jerusalem. Mark, Matthew and the twenty-first chapter of John indicate that Jesus first appeared to the eleven not in Jerusalem, but in Galilee. Whatever the divergences in the resurrection accounts may be, all evangelists are in agreement on two points. First, Jesus of Nazareth is risen! He has been seen by the disciples! Second, the resurrection of Jesus was a surprise. No one expected Jesus to rise from the dead.

Luke had his own special source for the Easter events narrated at the conclusion of his account of the good news. The experience of the women at the empty tomb differs considerably from the narrative found in Mark. The story of the two disciples on the road to Emmaus (24:13–35), the appearance of the risen Jesus in Jerusalem (24:36–49), and the ascension (24:50–53) are unique to Luke.

COMMENTARY. After Jesus had been taken down from the cross and entombed, the women prepared spices and perfumes for the body of the man they had faithfully followed from Galilee to Jerusalem (see 8:1–3; 23:55–56). The sabbath had interrupted their plans, so now, "very early on Sunday morning," the women return to complete the burial rites for their beloved Master (24:1). Finding the stone removed from the entrance of the grave, the women go inside. Luke is the only evangelist who relates that the women enter the tomb and discover the body of Jesus to be missing. They are puzzled (24:4). From their initial perspective, an empty tomb and a missing body was bad news. The body of Jesus should have been there. In view of the deep Jewish reverence for the dead and the religious duty to bury the dead properly, the absence of the body of Jesus meant trouble. Grave robbers or the enemies of Jesus could have stolen his body. But the angels, dressed in shining clothes (perhaps recalling the moment of Jesus' transfiguration in 9:29), ask the women a question that transforms their initial dejection to joy: "Why are you looking among the dead for one who is alive?" The women were in the place of death, looking for a corpse. The question gently reinterprets the meaning of the empty tomb. It is not that the body of Jesus has been stolen. He is not here because he is alive! The angels then explicitly state the joyful news: "He is not here; he has been raised" (24:6). This contrast between the dead and the living is Luke's basic perception of the meaning of resurrection (see also Jesus' reply to the Sadducees in 20:37–38).

While Mark's account tells us that the angel told the women to give Peter and the others the message that Jesus would meet them in Galilee (Mk 16:7), Luke seems to be in touch with another tradition, one that situates the appearances of the risen Jesus in Jerusalem. Thus Galilee is seen as the place where Jesus had foretold his death and resurrection:

> "Remember what he said to you while he was in Galilee: 'The Son of Man must be handed over to sinful men, be crucified, and three days later rise to life' " (24:6–7; see 9:18–22).

There is another Lucan connection between the resurrection and Jesus' first prophecy of his passion and death: the women who accompanied Jesus in Galilee (8:1–3) were among the disciples to whom Jesus spoke after Peter had acknowledged that Jesus was the Messiah: "Then Jesus gave *them* strict orders not to tell this to anyone. He also told *them*, 'The Son of Man must suffer much . . .' " (9:21–22). Because the women were disciples along with Jesus' male disciples, the angel tells the women at the tomb, "Remember what he said to *you* while he was in Galilee . . ." (24:6). Luke clearly wants it known that the same women who traveled with Jesus in Galilee (8:1–3) are also the ones who saw Jesus die (23:55). They are now given the mission of witnessing to Jesus' resurrection. They do remember his words (24:8) and go forth to "tell all *these things*" to the eleven and the others (24:9). Verse 9 thus links the women and the resurrection event with Luke's initial statement of purpose:

> *Dear Theophilus:*
> *Many people have done their best to write a report of the things that have taken place among us. They wrote what we have been told by those who saw these things from the beginning and who proclaimed the message (1:1–2).*

When Mary Magdalene, Joanna and Mary, mother of James, tell their experience to the apostles, the women are not believed (24:11). In our contemporary cultural outlook some of us tend to interpret verse 11 by projecting a male chauvinist attitude on to the apostles, as if they did not believe the news because the messengers were women. The truth of the matter, however, is that the apostles did not accept the witness of the women because the apostles did not expect Jesus to rise from the dead and were unwilling to believe that he did so. Peter, the leader of the apostles (see 5:10; 9:20; 22:31–32), ran to the tomb, saw the grave cloths, and went back to the others "amazed" but still lacking faith (24:12). The two disciples who set out for Emmaus also knew the story told by the women, but they did not believe that Jesus was risen any more than Peter did (24:22–24). In the remaining portion of his account Luke will tell how the other members of the community will move from amazement and perplexity to faith.

The Walk from Jerusalem to Emmaus and Back, 24:13–35

This event, recorded only by Luke, begins on the same day that the women discovered the empty tomb. Because Jerusalem is so central to Luke's understanding of God's plan of salvation, the very fact that these two disciples are journeying away from that city symbolizes that they are in the process of abandoning the journey they had begun as disciples of Jesus. (The situation may have spoken directly to those Gentile Christians who were tempted to give up their faith under the pressure of persecution.) As they talked about the events that had come to pass, Jesus himself joins them. Luke's reference to their being unable to recognize him (24:16) and his later statement regarding their eyes being opened (24:31) indicate that these disciples must make an interior journey from unbelief to faith in the risen Jesus.

There are two sections to this episode. The first deals with the dialogue between the two disciples and the unrecognized Jesus as they journey away from Jerusalem (24:15–27). The second portion contains the table dialogue that takes place in the village of Emmaus, where the two disciples and the risen Jesus share a meal (24:28–32). The first dialogue begins when the unrecognized Jesus joins Cleopas and the other disciple. (If Cleopas is a variant of Clopas, the husband of Mary mentioned in John 19:25, then the two disciples may have been husband and wife and the place where the meal was eaten may have been their home in Emmaus.) When Jesus asks about the subject of their conversation, Cleopas is surprised. With sad face that reflected his shattered hope and loss of faith, Cleopas wonders how this stranger could be ignorant of the events of the last few days (24:18). When Jesus asks "What things?" the reader is reminded of Luke's opening statement addressed to Theophilus (1:1–4). The explanation of the events given by Cleopas clearly indicates that he lacked faith in Jesus as God's suffering Messiah: "And we had hoped that he would be the one who was going to set Israel free!" (24:21). They had perceived Jesus as a great prophet who had met the same fate as other prophets. They had thought of their leader in terms of the popular messianic expectations, hoping that Jesus would be a nationalistic Messiah who would deliver Israel from Roman bondage. Their hopes shattered as deeply as their expectations for a triumphant Messiah had been ingrained, they left Jerusalem in spite of the report of the women that Jesus was alive (24:23–24).

Jesus emphatically responded: "How foolish you are, how slow you are to believe everything the prophets said!" (24:25). With the deepest conviction, the apparent stranger indicates that these two wayfarers should have realized that it was God's will that the Messiah was to suffer as he did. The force of the Greek expression is that of urgency; it is *necessary*, it *had* to come to pass as it did if the Messiah was to enter his glory (24:26)! We saw the same sense of events as part of God's plan in Jesus' first prophecy of his passion in 9:22. This is the moment, this is the event Jesus was preparing for during the whole of his life! "Didn't you know that I had to be in my Father's house?" (2:49) was the question Jesus asked of Mary and Joseph as a young man of twelve. To be in his Father's house is to be in his glory (24:26). Luke's account of the good news can be summarized in this movement of Jesus to his Father. Because these downcast disciples do not understand the mission God has given to his beloved servant-Son (see 3:22), the still-unrecognized Jesus goes through the Hebrew Scriptures, beginning with the five books of the law (Torah) given by Moses, and points out the passages that relate to the Messiah (24:27).

The stranger's explanations are such that the two disciples want him to stay longer; they prevail upon him to accept their hospitality. When the stranger blessed, broke and gave them the bread, their "eyes were opened," for they recognized him in the breaking of the bread (24:32). This is the climax of the Emmaus story—the recognition of Jesus in the breaking of the bread.

Note that Jesus uses the same gestures in 24:30 that he used when he shared bread with the five thousand (9:15–16) and when he celebrated the Passover meal with his apostles (22:19). On each occasion Jesus took the break in his hands, blessed it, broke it and gave the bread to others. In their recognition of Jesus in this ritual of giving thanks and eating, the two disciples are brought to complete faith. Jesus vanishes, but not before his little-faithed disciples (24:25) have made the connection between the Passover supper, his suffering and his rising to glory. Stirred by the unfolding of the meaning of the word of God (24:27) and sustained by the Eucharist, the two disciples immediately turn back to Jerusalem, the city of God's salvation (24:32–33).

They arrive, but before they can tell their story, they are greeted with the joyful message, "The Lord is risen indeed! He has appeared to Simon!" (24:34). This affirmation that Jesus is risen is the core of the Church's faith. Upon this assertion the entire New Testament depends (see 1 Cor 15:12–20). Luke's account of the Gospel has its starting point not at the birth of Jesus in Bethlehem, but at the resurrection of Jesus from the grave. Everything in this account of the good news has prepared the reader for this moment. Note that the message is not that "Jesus is risen" but *"the Lord* is risen." Not only has Peter seen his Master, he has also seen into the meaning of Jesus. Peter perceives that Jesus shares a unique relationship with God and that Jesus can be called Lord as the Father is Lord.

Only after the announcement of Simon Peter's revelatory encounter with Jesus do the two disciples have the chance to tell their experience of recognizing their "Lord" in the breaking of the bread. And now all is prepared for the last appearance of Jesus.

REFLECTION. Verses 25 through 32 reflect how the Eucharist was celebrated in the early years of the believing community. Note that it is evening, the time when the first century Christians commemorated the Lord's supper, when Jesus and the disciples share the meal. Prior to breaking bread, the early believers read the Scriptures and applied them to the life, death and resurrection of Jesus (see 24:25–27). The bread was then broken and shared (see 24:30–31). In the action of breaking bread Jesus was present (24:31).

We know that many first century believers, expecting the triumphant return of the Son of Man and the consequent end of the world, had been deeply disappointed. "Where is Jesus?" they puzzled. Luke saw that the Church was called to live in history, to journey in this world. So, in the story of the three wayfarers, Luke symbolically answered the question "Where is Jesus?" Luke recounted the story so that the believing community could know that Jesus is with us in the breaking of the bread. To this very day we believe that in the Eucharistic liturgy we encounter the crucified, risen and ascended Jesus who is sacramentally present. He is present in the consecrated bread; he is present in the liturgy of the world; he is present in the community, both individually and as the gathered assembly.

Even though the historical Jesus is no longer present to us in a visible way, the community is nevertheless filled with hope. He is gloriously risen! He has ascended to the Father! He has given us the pattern of discipleship—through suffering and death to eternal life in the kingdom of God! The reason why the disciple of Jesus finds the power to carry the cross daily (9:23), the reason why he or she carries it behind Jesus (23:26), is this: so that by imitating his life we may join him in resurrection. The Second Vatican Council often used the image of the pilgrim people of God to describe who we are as Church. It is appropriate to think of ourselves as wayfarers on the road to the heavenly Jerusalem. It is our privilege and destiny to enjoy already a taste of the kingdom (see 17:21) while we journey towards its fullness.

Jesus Appears to His Disciples, 24:36–49

OVERVIEW. Beginning with verse 36, the mood of the narration suddenly changes. Instead of joy there is fear and alarm (24:37). It seems that Luke wanted to stress what we might call "the sacramental presence" of Jesus in the recounting of the Emmaus story (24:13–35), but in the scene described in 24:36–43 Luke wanted to stress the physical reality of the risen Jesus in order to counter those who argued that the disciples merely saw a ghost (see 24:39–41). Note the similarity between this episode and John's recounting of Thomas' encounter with the risen Jesus. In that account Jesus said to Thomas, "Put your finger here; look, here are my hands. Give me your hand; put it into my side. Doubt no longer but believe" (Jn 20:27). Verses 44 through 48 summarize the Lucan account of the Gosepl. Verse 49 looks ahead toward the second volume of Luke's work, the Acts of the Apostles.

COMMENTARY. As the apostles and disciples gather for a meal, Jesus appears to them. What follows can be divided into two sections. The first section deals with the appearance of Jesus (24:36–43) and the second section contains Jesus' teaching about the fulfillment of the Scriptures and the commissioning of his followers to proclaim the good news to all nations (24:44–49).

In the first section Jesus appears suddenly. His greeting of peace (24:36) recalls the words that Gabriel spoke to Zechariah (1:12) and to Mary (1:30) at the beginning of Luke's account. However, in spite of Jesus' greeting, the disciples are terrified, alarmed and doubtful (24:37–38). Prior to this moment, Jesus had appeared to individuals. Now he presents himself to the official community. It is a climactic moment in which Jesus appears not after the manner of a ghost or an apparition, but in a body of flesh and bones (24:39), although transformed. To demonstrate his tangible reality, Jesus shows them his wounded hands and feet, still bearing the marks of his crucifixion (24:40; see Jn 20:20). The community of disciples is then described as so full of "joy and wonder" that they "still could not believe" (24:41). What is happening to them has gone far beyond any expectation they might have had, even beyond their imagining of what could happen. In his transformed existence Jesus would have no need for food, yet, for the sake of his disciples, he ate a piece of fish to demonstrate the authenticity of his bodily resurrection (24:42–43). The key concept in this section is the transformation of Jesus' existence through resurrection. He continued to have the same identity as he had before his crucifixion, including his body; he was not an apparition or ghost. However, resurrection went beyond mere resuscitation of a corpse. Jesus did not return to the same form of existence that he had before he was crucified. He now lives in a new realm of existence, but an existence that had continuity with the very same Jesus who had chosen his twelve apostles, traveled with his disciples, taught in the temple and died on the cross.

In the second section of Luke's recounting of Jesus' appearance to his assembled disciples (24:44–49), Jesus gives them his final instructions. Keep in mind that it is late Easter Sunday and that soon Jesus will depart (see 24:50–51). Since there is a definite unity between the Third Gospel and the Acts of the Apostles, and since Acts indicates that Jesus' departure took place forty days after his resurrection (Acts 1:3), we can view these six verses (24:44–49) as a summary of what Jesus taught his disciples during the forty day period after his resurrection.

Jesus begins (24:44) by referring to the words he spoke to his disciples when he was with them before his resurrection. He had then pointed out that the Son of Man would be put to death but rise three days later (9:22), that the Son of Man would be "handed over to the power of men" (9:44), that the Son of Man had to suffer and be rejected (17:25), and that in Jerusalem what the prophets foretold about the Son of Man would come true (18:31). The Hebrew Scriptures provide the basis for the explanation of the death and resurrection of Jesus (24:44). As he had opened the minds of the two disciples on the way to Emmaus (24:25–27), Jesus explains the meaning of the prophecies regarding the Messiah to the eleven disciples gathered together with the others (24:33):

> *This is what is written: the Messiah must suffer and must rise from death three days later, and in his name the message about repentance and the forgiveness of sins must be preached to all nations, beginning in Jerusalem. You are witnesses of these things (24:46–48).*

In the name of Jesus, the Messiah, the disciples are charged to proclaim to all nations that repentance leads to the joy of having one's sins forgiven (24:47). The phrase "in his name" conveys the notion of power and authority and suggests the text of Daniel in which the Son of Man "was given authority, honor, and royal power, so that the people of all nations, races, and languages would serve him" (Dan 7:13–14).

Those Gentile Christians for whom Luke wrote could easily recognize themselves as the beneficiaries of the mission that Jesus gave to his disciples after his resurrection. That mission began in Jerusalem (24:47) and would be carried to Judea, to Samaria, and "to the ends of the earth" (Acts 1:8). The stress on Jerusalem throughout Luke's account of the Gospel, including Jerusalem's being the city from which the good news would be preached to all nations, brings to mind the vision of Isaiah concerning Jerusalem:

> In the days to come,
> the mountain of the Lord's house
> shall be established as the highest mountain
> and raised above the hills.
> All nations shall stream toward it;
> many people shall come and say:
> "Come, let us climb the Lord's mountain,
> to the house of the God of Jacob.
> That he may instruct us in his ways,
> and we may walk in his paths."
> For from Zion shall go forth instructions,
> and the word of the Lord from Jerusalem.
> He shall judge between the nations,
> and impose terms on many peoples.
> They shall beat their swords into plowshares

and their spears into pruning hooks;
One nation shall not raise the sword against another,
nor shall they train for war again (Is 2:2–5, NAB).

When Jesus asserts that the eleven and the other disciples are *"witnesses of these things"* (24:48), the reader is again reminded of Luke's statement of purpose at the beginning of his work: "Many people . . . wrote what we have been told by those *who saw these things* from the beginning and who proclaimed the message" (1:1–2). In the room that Easter evening were the eleven apostles and many other disciples, among whom were most likely the women who had followed Jesus from Galilee (see 8:2–3; 23:55) and Mary, the model disciple (see 8:21; Acts 1:14).

Luke closely linked the disciples' commission to witness with the Father's promise of the power from above (24:49). The Spirit who has inspired and guided Jesus throughout his ministry (see 3:22; 4:1, 18) will be given to the disciples on the appointed day (24:49; Acts 2:1–4). But first Jesus must finish his journey to his Father.

Jesus Is Taken Up to Heaven, 24:50–53

In 9:51 Jesus had resolutely decided to "set out on his way to Jerusalem." In this way he began the one long journey to the city where he was martyred. Now, as Jesus blesses his disciples and ascends to his Father (24:50–51), that journey is truly complete.

Luke's account of the good news finishes with a certain symmetry. At the beginning of the Third Gospel, Zechariah, mute after his encounter with the angel Gabriel, was unable to give the customary blessing to the people gathered in the temple (1:21–22). At the end of the Gospel Jesus raises his hands and blesses his disciples as he departs (24:51). In the temple, the very place where Luke began his account of the Gospel (1:9), he brings it to a conclusion. There, constantly, the disciples of Jesus rejoice and praise God (24:53).